GOD'S LAW
AND GOD'S LOVE

GOD'S LAW
AND GOD'S LOVE

An Essay in Comparative Religion

NORMAN ANDERSON

COLLINS
ST JAMES'S PLACE, LONDON
1980

William Collins Sons & Co Ltd
London · Glasgow · Sydney · Auckland
Toronto · Johannesburg

The author and publishers wish to acknowledge
the following publications and publishers:
The Rainbird Publishing Group, London
(*Concise Encyclopedia of Living Faiths*)
SCM Press, London (*Dictionary of Christian Theology*);
Hodder & Stoughton, London and The Seabury Press, New York
(Davis, *Christ and the World Religions*);
Hodder & Stoughton, London and Oxford University Press, New York
(Blanch, *Trumpet in the Morning*);
Inter-Varsity Press, Leicester
(Leurer, 'Judaism', *The World's Religions*
and Wenham and Barclay, *Law, Morality and the Bible*);
Oxford University Press, Oxford
(Zaehner, *Hinduism* and Neill, *Christian Faith and Other Faiths*);
James Clark & Co., Cambridge
(Underhill, *Mystics of the Church*).

First published 1980
Copyright © Sir Norman Anderson 1980
ISBN 0 00 215296 7
Made and printed in Great Britain by
T. J. Press (Padstow) Ltd, Padstow, Cornwall

Contents

Foreword

Surprising as it may seem, at a time when – in the Western world – churchgoing is on the wane and institutional religion has lost much of its influence, questions which lie at the heart of man's religious instinct evoke what seems to be an increasing interest. Is there a God? What is he like? Is there any fundamental difference between the great world religions, or are they basically the same? Do they conceive of God – or the Ultimate Reality – in terms of law, or love, or both? And how do they reconcile their beliefs with the facts of life and human experience?

Some time ago I received an invitation to give the Henry Drummond Lectures for 1979 in the University of Stirling, with the tentative suggestion that 'perhaps three topics in the area of Law and Comparative Religion might be appropriate'. This struck me at first as a somewhat strange combination of subjects – for law and comparative religion do not seem to be natural bed-fellows – proposed by the Trustees, *ad hominem*, to accord with my own interests and qualifications. This may well be true; for, after reading law at Cambridge, I had served in the Arab world first as a missionary and then in the Forces, had spent some thirty years studying, teaching and writing about Islamic Law as it is applied today in the Middle East, Africa and Asia, and had also done a good deal of speaking and writing about the Christian faith – sometimes as seen by a lawyer, and sometimes in relation to other religions. But it soon dawned on me that the proposed subjects were not nearly as disparate

as they might seem, for all religions take a vital interest in
the concept of some Law which, they believe, lies behind the
phenomena of nature and the obligations of human life and
behaviour — whether they regard this Law as a pattern of
transcendental principles of a largely impersonal nature or
as the design and directions of a personal Creator. Yet they
differ profoundly, of course, not only in their concept of the
nature of that Law, but in the place they believe it to hold in
the meaning of human life and the sum total of what all of
them, in their own distinctive ways, regard as 'salvation'.

To approach religion in terms of the law of God without
the complementary concept of the love of God would, however, be very one-sided, and I was intrigued to find that, in
his Preface to *Natural Law in the Spiritual World* (at least
in its twenty-seventh edition!), Drummond had himself
quoted Browning's words:

'I spoke as I saw.
I report, as a man may of God's work
— *all's Love and all's Law.*'

But this quotation brings us face to face with a very different attitude from one that is widely prevalent today, for
we live in a world in which law and love are more often
regarded as in antithesis to each other than in harmony, let
alone anything remotely approaching identity. Law is commonly thought of as cold, calculating, exacting and con-
demnatory, while love is welcomed as warm, spontaneous,
generous and compassionate. The antithesis between them
is seen most clearly if we substitute 'legalism' for 'law', or if
we depict the typical lawyer as precise, pedantic and hair-
splitting. This is, of course, a caricature — yet one which
leaves the features it distorts sufficiently recognizable! But,
however this may be, there is no doubt which we should
choose — law or love — if we were compelled to opt for one or
the other.

Much of this reaction, however, rests on a misapprehension. To begin with, no theist can view God's work of creation as other than a manifestation of his love; and the same is true of the structure and laws of that creation, both physical and spiritual — marred although some of these are, as we see them today, by the intrusion of human, and even cosmic, sin. It is almost inconceivable, moreover, that a beneficent Creator would not have bequeathed to his rational creatures what we might term their 'Maker's Directions' as to how they should live and could find their true happiness and fulfilment. Even among men it is a misconception to regard the primary function of law as restraint and limitation rather than protection and liberation, although it is obvious that, in a very imperfect world, it is impossible to protect those who need protection without imposing some restraints on those who would otherwise exploit their vulnerability. But the basic purpose of law is the welfare of the community — which is also, of course, the goal of love.[1]

The Henry Drummond Lectures were established quite recently in Stirling, the city of his birth — by a happy agreement between the Trustees and the University — to commemorate a scholar, evangelist and writer who had a widespread influence, especially in the student world, a century ago. I am most grateful to both the Trustees and the University for the invitation to give these lectures, and to the staff and students — and, especially, to the Principal and Mrs Crammond — for the generous hospitality that my wife and I enjoyed during our visit. It was obviously impossible, however, to do more than begin to open up a vast subject in

---

[1] This is *not*, however, to accept Joseph Fletcher's statements that 'Love and justice are the same, for justice is love distributed, nothing else', or that love and justice 'are one and the same thing, and *cannot* vary' — for this evacuates both terms of any precise meaning. Cf. his *Situation Ethics* (SCM Press, London, 1966), pp. 87 and 89.

the course of only three lectures, so I am greatly indebted to the publishers William Collins for encouraging me to deal with the subject a little more adequately in this book. I am also exceedingly grateful to the Reverend H. St J. Hart, Fellow and former Dean of Queens' College, Cambridge, and to the Reverend N. T. Wright, Fellow and Chaplain of Downing College, for their kindness in reading this book in typescript and giving me the much valued benefit of their criticism and advice. Needless to say, I alone am responsible for the defects that remain.

NORMAN ANDERSON
Cambridge, November 1979

CHAPTER I

The Law of God and the Love of God in Eastern Religions and Western Thought

It is a comparatively straightforward task to analyse the place given to the twin concepts of the law of God and the love of God in Judaism, Islam and Christianity, but a much more difficult problem in regard to the great religions of the East. There can, however, be no country which has been so deeply characterized by religious practices and philosophical systems as has India, in which Hinduism evolved over so many centuries and both Jainism and Buddhism had their birth. Hinduism and Buddhism, moreover, claim so many adherents today – the first primarily in India, and the second throughout Asia – that their importance in any study of comparative religion is indisputable. But both religions have, with the passage of the years, undergone so many transformations in their beliefs and diversifications in their philosophical views that they demand a lifetime of specialist study, to say nothing of linguistic expertise. So I cannot hope, in this chapter, to do more than provide a bare introduction to a very abstruse and complicated subject.

The nub of the problem from the point of view of our present study, however, is the fact that Jainism is explicitly atheistic,[1] Buddhism in its Theravāda form implicitly atheistic,[2] and

---

[1] Cf. M. Hiriyanna, *The Essentials of Indian Philosophy* (Allen & Unwin, London, 1949), p. 59.   [2] Cf. Christmas Humphreys, *Buddhism* (Penguin Books, London, 3rd ed., 1962), p. 79.

11

the Advaita Vedānta school of Hindu philosophy explicitly monistic in its teaching;[3] and, while each of these views of Ultimate Reality may, no doubt, recognize certain 'laws' as having transcendental significance (which is one reason why I have included in this chapter the concept of Natural Law as this has been developed in the West), it is exceedingly difficult to see how 'love' can be ascribed to an impersonal Reality. But, however this may be, it is clear that the majority of Hindus believe in a personal God or gods, and that Buddhism in its Mahāyāna form may be thought to approximate to some sort of theism, so we must attempt to understand the basic beliefs of those who follow these religions. Our starting point, moreover, must be Hinduism, from which both Jainism and Buddhism sprang.

There is a bewildering plethora of Hindu sacred writings which are regarded as having different degrees of authority or 'inspiration'. The earliest is the Veda (a word which means 'knowledge'). There are, in fact, four such compilations, each of which is made up of Mantras (hymns), Brāhmaṇas (liturgical writings) and Upanishads (secret teaching). These are all classed as *śruti* (hearing) and believed to be the eternal word heard by sages of immemorial memory.[4] They were followed, considerably later, by the Sūtras, which are largely made up of aphorisms which summarize the teaching of the Veda according to the interpretation accepted by the different schools of philosophy, and the Mahābhārata – a gigantic epic which includes the famous Bhagavad-Gītā, or 'Song of the Lord'. These were accorded the lower status of smṛti (tradition); but the Gītā, in particular, has had a profound influence.[5] It is to this period that *The Laws of Manu*, the most authoritative of Hindu law books, may be assigned.[6]

---

[3] Cf. Hiriyanna, *op. cit.*, pp. 152 ff.   [4] *Ibid*, pp. 9 f., 14 ff., 18 ff., and 44 f.   [5] *Op. cit.*, pp. 31 f., 36 ff., 44 f., etc.   [6] Cf. R. C. Zaehner, *Hinduism*, (OUP, 1966), p. 109.

But in order to get a lucid picture of the way in which Hinduism has developed down the ages (and, indeed, the bewildering mixture and interaction of several different strands in that religion which prevail today) it will be helpful at this point, I think, to summarize four periods in its long history as these have been analysed by Professor R. C. Zaehner.[7]

(1) The earliest period, that of the Veda, was 'frankly polytheistic and clearly akin to the religions of other Indo-European nations', although it is now known that much that has come down to us from this period is in fact pre-Aryan in origin.[8]

(2) Next, this developed into a 'pantheistic monism' in which

> The All is seen as centred on the One or is wholly identified with the One: in its extreme form the individual human soul is identified with the Absolute. In effect this means that the gods are dethroned and the human soul is set up in their place. This is the form of Hinduism recently revived in India itself and far beyond her borders in the Western world which lays all its stress on *moksha*, the liberation of the human soul from time, space and matter.[9]

(3) The third phase (which Zaehner regards as 'perhaps the most important') is the development within Hinduism of strong monotheistic trends on the one hand and the crystallization and ossification of the caste system on the other.

> Preoccupation with the liberation of the soul from the bondage of time and matter gives way to a rapt adoration of God, that is to say, of the great traditional gods, Vishnu and Śiva, now regarded by their devotees

---

[7] *Op. cit.*, pp. 6-9.   [8] Cf. Hiriyanna, *op. cit.*, pp. 10-17.
[9] Cf. Hiriyanna, *op. cit.*, pp. 18-29 and 50 f.

as the supreme Reality and absolute Lord. This religion of loving devotion or *bhakti* became the real religion of the mass of the people and has remained so ever since. It was not easy to fit into the general scheme of classical Hinduism with its almost deterministic view of the phenomenal world and its stress on *moksha* as the final end of man. . . .[10]

It has, he insists, too often been said that Hinduism as such regards the world as an illusion. But this has never been true of Hinduism as a whole — whether of its sacred writings or of popular religion. It is characteristic of only one of six schools of philosophy, although currently the dominant one. Nevertheless

it is true to say that there is and, except in the very earliest period, always has been a double tension within the Hindu religion — the striving after liberation from this world which all admit to be the final goal of man on the one hand and man's obligation to do what is right *in* this world on the other, the tension between *moksha* and *dharma* — and in the second instance the tension between two types of *dharma*, the *sanātana dharma* or absolute moral order which can never be precisely defined yet is felt to have absolute validity, and the *dharma* of caste and canon law as laid down in the various law-books. These tensions are most plainly exhibited in India's Great Epic, the *Mahābhā-rata*, which sums up within its vast bulk every shade and nuance of classical Hinduism, both its orthodox formulations and the outraged protests that these evoked.

(4)   The fourth phase of Hinduism, through which we are living today, is, he says, the denial of its formal self and the reassertion of its spiritual essence.

[10] Cf. Hiriyanna, *op. cit.*, pp. 32-36 and 175-197.

This revaluation of Hinduism was prepared by the reform movements of the nineteenth century, but only reached and touched the hearts of the entire Indian people with the advent of . . . Mahātma Gandhi. For it was he who lent his enormous prestige to the onslaught on what all that was finest in India had for centuries felt to be a canker in the very heart of their religion, the caste system and its ugly corollary, the creation of a disfranchised religious proletariat, the outcastes or untouchables. Gandhi exposed the glaring discrepancy between the two *dharmas*, the 'eternal law' that is 'so difficult to know' but which was inscribed on India's social conscience and what was now seen to be a manmade *dharma* that gave its sanction to a social system which had developed into something monstrously unjust. The tension that through the centuries had existed between the two *dharmas* was brutally exposed to the light of day; and it is no accident that Gandhi met his death at the hand of an orthodox Hindu.

Now what does all this mean in terms of Hindu thought today in so far as the law and love of God are concerned? Hinduism is essentially a religion of law or duty – and, in spite of the influence of Gandhi and other reformers, there are still plenty of orthodox Hindus whose devotion to the caste system is both inherent and instinctive, who regard the law of their caste as paramount and binding and whose attachment to the concept of a *sanātana dharma* is largely confined to the use of that term as a synonym for their religion as such. Whether one can properly regard *dharma* (of whatever variety) as the equivalent of the law of *God* depends first, of course, on whether the people concerned believe in a personal divine Being, or even a multiplicity of such beings, rather than an abstract Reality or impersonal Principle; and, secondly, on whether it is possible to equate

a law which is conceived to be part of the essential and
eternal nature of things as in some sense the 'Law of God'
even when those who believe in it are agnostic, or definitely
atheistic, in their attitude to a personal Deity. This is a subject to which we shall soon have to return. But, however this
may be, there is in Hinduism an obvious connection (however, precisely, it may be expressed) between the key concepts of *dharma* (duty) and *karma* (religious rite, or 'action'
in general: especially action appropriate to a person of one's
particular caste). There is, indeed, a sense in which *karma*
is thought of as without beginning and without end, for
Hindus believe that every action is the effect of actions
which have gone before and will itself inevitably give rise to
further actions in the future. In another (but allied) sense a
man's *karma* is regarded as a sort of chain round his neck
leading him inevitably to his next incarnation – which may,
accordingly, be higher or lower in the scale of humanity, or
even as a celestial being, an animal or a reptile. This concept is absolutely fundamental to Hinduism: for, unless this
chain of cause and effect can somehow be broken, there can
be no end to a perpetual round of birth, death and rebirth.
No wonder, then, that *moksha*, or release from this apparently endless sequence,[11] is the goal to which Hindu piety
looks forward. The Upanishads teach, moreover,

> that the human soul in its deepest essence is in
> some sense identical with Brahman, the unchanging
> something that is yet the source of all change. This
> soul, then, must be distinct from the ordinary em-
> pirical self which transmigrates from body to body
> carrying its load of *karma* with it. How to realize this
> eternal soul and how to disengage it from its real or

[11] Technically known as *saṁsāra*, or 'the "course" or "revolution" to which
all phenomenal existence is subject, and which is itself subject to and conditioned by an endless causal past, the *dharma* of the universe'. (Zaehner,
op. cit., p. 4).

imaginary connection with the psychosomatic complex that thinks, wills, and acts, is from the time of the Upanishads onwards the crucial problem facing the Hindu religious consciousness.[12]

But, whatever may be said about the philosophical development of Hinduism, the religion of most simple villagers even today can basically be regarded as a species of polytheism; and to the mind of the polytheist there are gods who are good and others who are evil, gods who are benevolent and others who are malignant. To more sophisticated persons, on the other hand, Hinduism represents a form of monotheistic – or, more precisely, henotheistic – religion: that is, the worship of a God who reveals himself in a variety of different forms – whether in what are termed *avatārs*, or mythological 'descents' in the guise of men or animals, or in the ordinary phenomena of nature. In any case, however, both good and evil are regarded as created by, and proceeding directly from, the same God. There are, it is true, glimpses of the concept of a 'saviour-god' in the pictures of Krishna in the Gītā – as may be seen in the stories of how he saved cowherds, on several occasions, from a forest fire that had surrounded them and was threatening to suffocate them. According to this school of thought, moreover, it is only through God's grace that 'the *karma* attaching to a soul can be cancelled out and that it can "become Brahman" and through becoming Brahman be in a fit state to draw near to God'.[13]

This opened the door, in some measure at least, to the various *bhakti* movements of loving devotion to a personal God which have sprung up from time to time in different parts of India. In Hindu literature the Gītā forms part of the Great Epic to which reference has already been made; and this claims to be part of the 'fifth Veda'. But at much the same time, perhaps in the fourth century AD, a whole mass

[12] Zaehner, *op. cit.*, p. 60.   [13] *Ibid.*, p. 96.

of new sacred literature was taking shape. This literature is known as the *Purānas*, forms part of the non-Vedic scripture known as *smṛti*, and finds much of its religious importance in the *Bhāgavata Purāna* which was probably compiled in the ninth century. In this the central figure is Krishna, as an *avatār* of Vishnu. Brought up among the cowherds he sported with their daughters, the *gopīs*, who became distraught with love of him; and this became the symbol of the love of the human soul for God. What is much more to our point, however, is the concept that this is not exclusively one-sided, for God is in love with the human soul. 'In this divine love-affair', indeed, 'God is necessarily the male, the soul the female: God takes the initiative and the soul must passively wait for the divine embrace.'[14]

It was in the Tamil lands of South India that the cult of Krishna first came into prominence, for there a considerable spiritual revival was initiated, at least by the eighth century, by persons describing themselves as 'Ālvārs', or 'men who have an intuitive knowledge of God'. To Rāmānuja, who was strongly influenced by the Ālvārs, *moksha* was 'only the *via purgativa* which precedes the *via contemplativa* in which all action is left to God, his grace, and his love; the soul can do no more than yearn that God will have mercy on it, and long and bitter though the intervening stages of aridity may be, the soul knows that God cannot in the end but be merciful, however sinful it may be'.[15]

It was in the Tamil lands that the cult of Śiva, too, first developed. There were a number of excesses, but the cult soon spread throughout India. It was the work 'of a series of saints who spread the gospel that salvation could only be won by a total self-surrender to Śiva'; and the Śaivite hymns which they produced

    are distinguished from their Vaishnavite counterparts

[14] *Ibid.*, p. 127.   [15] *Ibid.*, pp. 127-129.

by the extreme sense of unworthiness that the devotee feels in the face of the all-holiness of God. The philosopy of the *Śaiva-Siddhānta* . . . is based as much on the Śvetāśvatara Upanishad as it is on the writings of the Tamil saints, but it was the influence of the latter that made the writers of the *Śaiva-Siddhānta* attach such enormous importance to the doctrine of grace freely given and the impossibility of spiritual progress without love. The whole movement is an impassioned cry against the ossified ceremonial religion of the Brāhmans and the ideal of 'passionlessness' that they shared with the Buddhists and the Jains.[16]

But what 'distinguishes the Tamil Śaivite saints from almost all the other *bhakti* cults is their intense sense of personal guilt; man, as he exists apart from God, is evil and horribly corrupt'.[17]

The *Bhagavad-Gītā*, which represents only a tiny part of the Mahābhārata, is almost certainly India's best loved religious classic. But it is only at the very end that God's love for man is clearly stated in the words:

Hear again the most secret [doctrine] of all, my ultimate word. Because I greatly desire thee, therefore shall I tell thee thy salvation. Think on me, worship me, sacrifice to me, pay me homage, so shalt thou come to me. I promise thee truly, for I love thee well. Give up all the things of *dharma*, turn to me only as thy refuge. I will deliver thee from all evil. Have no care.[18]

But it was not till the time of Rāmānuja, in the eleventh century, that the significance of these words was given full

---

[16] *Ibid.*, pp. 130 f.   [17] *Ibid.*, p. 132. It is noteworthy that Professor A. L. Basham states that 'Some authorities would claim that Tamil Śaivism is the highest form of Hindu devotional religion (*The Concise Encyclopedia of Living Faiths* (Hutchinson, London, 2nd. ed., 1977), p. 227).   [18] *Ibid.*, p. 98.

emphasis, as when he declared that God

> is an ocean of boundless compassion, moral excellence,
> tenderness, generosity, and sovereignty, the refuge of
> the whole world. . . . He, the one ocean of tenderness
> to all who resort to him, takes away the sorrows of his
> devotees.

Indeed, God is represented as saying: 'Whoever loves me
beyond measure, him will I love beyond measure [in
return]. Unable to bear separation from him, I cause him to
possess me. This is my true promise: you will come to me.'[19]
So, in Rāmānuja's teaching, the soul in the liberated state is
neither annihilated nor absorbed, but experiences unending
and ever-increasing love.

But this is only one aspect — and a very special aspect — of
Hindu teaching. At least equally typical, I think, is the
description that Klaus Klostermaier gave, after a close and
sympathetic study of contemporary Hinduism in Vrindaban, of an incident in which he saw a goat die of sunstroke
and then be torn to pieces first by vultures, then by dogs,
and finally by jackals. 'God', he wrote,

> was the creator and preserver and destroyer. The
> reason for placing creatures in a desert, in a cruel
> world, in death — that was his caprice, his play, his lila.
> First he had created the sun who would one day kill the
> goat he had also created. He had created the vultures
> who would consume the goat. The dogs and jackals
> who would tear the skin to pieces and crack the bones
> with their teeth, they also were his creatures. *One*
> atman[20] in all of them — in God and in the vulture, in

[19] *Ibid.*, p. 99.   [20] The terms Brahman and Ātman form a sort of
equation in Hindu thought. In the Advaita Vedānta view, for example,
Brahman stands for 'the unchanging ground of the universe' and Ātman
for 'the innermost essence or Inner Self of man' — which this school of
thought regards as identical. Cf. Charles Davis, *Christ and the World
Religions*, (Hodders, London, 1979), p. 105.

the goat and in the dog. And also in the one who
watched all this, trying to understand. God was the
kind mother — and the bloodthirsty goddess of destruction. When misfortune goes on increasing, when catastrophe breaks all bounds, it is imperative to sacrifice to
the goddess; her long tongue hangs bloodthirstily from
her mouth, she holds a bloodstained sword, cut-off
heads and arms are hanging decoratively over her
naked breasts. Life issues from God's countenance —
death from his back. God is the sacrificer and the
sacrifice. Goat and vulture are his manifestations —
adoration are due to both.[21]

Now it is clear that in this quotation a pantheistic and
henotheistic view of Hinduism come very close together. On
the first view all the actors and phenomena are actually part
of the deity, while on the other they are different manifestations of his nature. On either view, I can see that 'adoration' may be regarded as 'due' to all if the term is used
purely in the sense of the acknowledgement of a divine
status — although I must confess that I find the idea distinctly repugnant. But if the word 'adoration' is used in the
sense of profound love, then the requirement clearly
becomes impossible. For love cannot be forced, but must
either be won or arise spontaneously.

In any case, we are concerned not with the love of man for
God but the love of God for man. Admittedly the phrase 'the
love of God' can, by itself, be construed both ways, either as
a subjective or an objective genitive. Biblical commentators
continually have to make this observation, and then come
down on one side or the other. But in this case any such
question is clearly foreclosed by the phrase 'The law of
God' — for this must mean the law that God has promul-

[21] *Hindu and Christian in Vrindaban* (SCM Press, London, 1969), p. 46.
I have previously made use of this quotation in my *Christianity and Comparative Religion* (Tyndale Press, London, 1970), p. 77.

gated for his creatures, rather than any 'law' that applies to
his own being. And in this sense, while it might of course be
said that he showed 'love' to the vultures, dogs and jackals by
providing them with food, the quotation as a whole — and,
in particular, the latter part of it — would seem to preclude
any concept of a God whose basic nature is love.

Yet this, again, is only one side of a very complex picture.
In spite of the dominance, among the intellectual elite, of
philosophical interpretations of Hinduism which are monistic or atheistic,[22] the majority of Hindus certainly think of
God — or the gods — in much more personal terms. Even so,
any emphasis on his (or their) love for man seems to be
largely confined to the more fervent *bhakti* circles, and to
the writings of men like Nāmm'alvār, Tukārām and,
especially, Rāmānuja. But Hinduism is not so much one
religion as a whole compendium of religions and philosophies, into which alien influences may very easily in-
filtrate; and it would appear distinctly possible that the far
from typical views of some of these devotees — and especially
the intense sense of personal guilt which appears to be
unique to Tamil-speaking Śaivites — may, in part at least,
represent some such borrowing. In general, it certainly
seems clear that Hinduism basically represents a religion of
'law' rather than love, with the concepts of *dharma* and
karma occupying a central position.

As we have seen, the term *dharma* does not only stand for
law, but for duty and right action, and a soul's future
depends on the *karma* it carries with it to its next rebirth. In
the case of those Hindus who believe in a personal God, it
may be true to say that

> his ultimate purpose is the final liberation of all souls
> from the trammels of matter which is itself his own
> 'lower nature'. He binds that he may loose and that he
> may lead all souls back to himself whether they like it

[22] Cf. pp. 24 ff. and 138 ff. below.

or not.[23] This is the eternal 'game' that he plays with his creation; but like any game it has its own rules, and the rules of the game are called *dharma*. God alone knows the rules, but he can and does on occasion reveal them to man as Krishna[24] did to Arjuna, and man, in his turn, obeys the rules willy-nilly, for he is conditioned by his own *karma* – the works that follow him from lives lived long ago into his present life with the same blind instinct that enables the calf to find the mother-cow wherever she may be in the herd. . . . Arjuna may not understand with his finite intellect why a fratricidal war involving the slaughter of millions is both necessary and right and therefore part and parcel of 'eternal *dharma*' itself, but loath though he may be to take his cousins' lives he is not in fact a free agent, and must. However wrong the *dharma* imposed on you by your caste and by circumstances may appear to you, you are none the less bound to do it.[25]

Yet, as has been noted in passing, some Hindus have come, in much agony of soul, to make a distinction (vividly depicted in the mythological story of Yudhishthira, whom Charles Davis describes as 'the personification of dharma'[26] between the *dharma* of their particular caste, as taught by the Brāhmans and even the 'divine' Krishna, and the eternal or '*sanātana dharma*', to which progressive Hindus and Indian reformers tend increasingly to appeal – whether they are in fact thinking in terms of some human formulation of principles (like the Universal Declaration of Human Rights or, indeed, parts of their own Indian Constitution), or in terms of that basic sense of what is right or wrong which, St

---

[23] This is, perhaps, as near as *most* Hinduism gets to the concept of divine love.   [24] In one of the *avatārs* of Vishnu, in which he instructs Arjuna, a member of the warrior-caste, about *dharma*.   [25] Zaehner, *op. cit.*, p. 103.   [26] *Christ and the World Religions* (Hodder & Stoughton, London, 1970), p. 106.

Paul tells us, is in some part 'written' on the human heart as such.[27] But, however that may be, the Hindu equivalent for 'salvation' is the concept of *moksha*, which does not basically mean liberation from moral guilt but from the human condition as such (and, in particular, from the *saṁsāric* process of continual reincarnation — whether as men, gods or animals — according to the law of *karma*). To the Advaita Vedānta school of thought (which is still the dominant philosophical creed of the intellectual elite) this means the union of the individual soul with the Eternal Soul; and this, in their view, is already a basic reality, so all that is needed is for man to come to a full realization of this fact — although they commonly admit that this is unlikely to take place before he has passed through a considerable series of reincarnations. This realization leads to a tranquil peace in which, as the Māndūkya Upanishad puts it, the soul

> has cognizance neither of what is inside nor what is outside, nor of both together. . . . It is unseen; there can be no commerce with it; it is impalpable, has no characteristics, unthinkable; it cannot be designated. Its essence is its firm conviction of the oneness of itself; it causes the phenomenal world [*māyā*] to cease; it is tranquil and mild, devoid of duality.[28]

This is the position to which Śankara firmly adhered. To him and to the true Advaitin, therefore, *moksha*

> does not mean that the soul merges into Brahman as a river merges into the sea, but that it realizes itself as it eternally is, that is, as the One Brahman-Ātman, which is Absolute Being, Consciousness and Bliss. With the realization of this, *māyā* disappears and is shown to be totally unreal. Real and verifiable from

[27] Romans 2:15. There is, however, much disagreement regarding whether this verse refers to all men, or only to Christians under the New Covenant. Cf. C. E. B. Cranfield, *Romans* (Vol. I, 6th ed., Edinburgh, 1975).   [28] Quoted by Zaehner, *op. cit.*, p. 56.

the point of view of the soul still in bondage to matter, it is unreal to the soul which has realized the true oneness of itself.[29]

Śankara, then, 'does not deny the existence of the Creator God on the empirical level nor does he identify the soul with this God on any level. Creation, omnipotence and omniscience are the attributes of God as seen by man while still in the bondage of *māyā*. . . . Dependence, limited knowledge, and limited power are among the attributes of the man not yet liberated. . . . But from the absolute point of view *māyā* does not exist.[30] This means, of course, that whereas God and man are distinct on the relative level, in reality they are completely identical; and this is what *moksha* reveals.

The Sāmkhya philosophy is almost entirely different. Here the goal is not 'to see all things in the self and the self in all things', but rather to *isolate* the individual self or soul from all other things – whether the *samsāric* world or all other souls which, like itself, are 'self-subsisting and autarchic monads'. Whereas the Advaita Vedānta system is rigidly monist, therefore, the Sāmkhya philosophy (like the Yoga system, which so closely resembles it that the two are often known as the 'Sāmkhya-Yoga') is emphatically dualist. This is partly why the Sāmkhya-Yogins reject the essential unity of the individual 'self' with any universal, all-pervading self or World Soul – the very existence of which they deny.[31] Where the Advaita Vedānta and Sāmkhya-Yoga systems do agree is in the absolute distinction between the temporal and the eternal; for the 'starting point both of Śankara and the Sāmkhya-Yoga is the *experience* of the immortality of the soul'; and immortality in this case does not mean the infinite prolongation of human life in time: that is *samsāra* which the Hindus regard

---

[29] Zaehner, *op. cit.*, p. 76.   [30] *Ibid.*, p. 77. cf. Hiriyanna, *op. cit.*, pp. 160 ff.   [31] Cf. Zaehner, *op. cit.*, pp. 69 f; Hiriyanna, *op. cit.*, pp. 106 ff.

rather as a living death; it is death-in-life, not life-in-death. It means rather an unconditioned and absolutely static condition which knows nothing of time and space and upon which death has no hold; and because it is not only pure Being, but also pure consciousness and pure bliss, it must be analagous to life. It is, then, life-in-death: it has the immobility of death but the consciousness of life.[32]

Two points must be noted here in the interests of clarity. First, the term Yoga is used not only of one of the six philosophical schools of Hinduism in its own right, but of 'the physical, mental, and psychic technique practised in India by followers of the major philosophical schools either for purely spiritual purposes or in order to produce maximal physical, mental, and spiritual well-being'. When, moreover, reference is made to the Sāṁkhya-Yoga as a single system, this is not only because the two philosophies are so closely akin, but also because Sāṁkhya is regarded as 'supplying the theoretical basis and Yoga the technique for achieving the highest goal envisaged by the Sāṁkhya, that is, the total *isolation* of the individual monad which is the soul from all other souls and from the whole domain of Nature'. The second point which needs clarification follows from the fact that in the second stage of the Yoga system the phrase 'devotion to God' is mentioned — which seems in direct contradiction to the assertion that neither the Sāṁkhya nor the Yoga system have any place for union with God. But Zaehner explains this apparent anomaly by saying that this 'god'

is no different from other souls in that he is eternal and unlimited by time, since that is the natural condition of all souls, but he *is* different from them in that he is never affected by matter or Nature. . . . *Moksha*, then, for the *Sāṁkhya-Yogin*, means to become *like* God in

[32] Zaehner, *op. cit.*, p. 74.

his timeless unity, it does not mean to participate with him in any way.[33]

Buddhism, which of course sprang from Hinduism, has also manifested a wide diversity of forms. In Theravāda (or Hīnayāna) Buddhism,[34] for example, the Buddha is the historical Gautama who became the Enlightened One, the supreme teacher and example, and the exemplification of *Nirvāṇa* (a state of passionless peace). It is easy enough to regard Gautama's teaching about how others, too, can reach this goal as a form of 'law', in the widest sense of that term — particularly in the light of the Theravādin's insistence that there can be no outside help in regard to the *karma* (of merit or demerit) which each individual has accumulated. It is also perfectly fair to consider Gautama himself an example of love — since, after 'attaining *Nirvāṇa*', he made the noble choice of setting out on a wandering mission to instruct those who were still in darkness. But it is very difficult indeed to argue that Theravādins teach either the law or love of a *God* whose very existence — even in the form of an impersonal Absolute or Supreme Soul — they (in company with the Jains) refuse to acknowledge. All they will admit is an 'extra-temporal something that inheres in all human souls — something left more or less undefined by the Buddhists but classified as an atomic monad by the Jains'.[35]

I suppose it is *just* possible to regard a law which they believe to emanate, in some way, from the transcendent as an approximation to what theists would call the law of God; but it is virtually impossible to discern any concept whatever of the love of God in a doctrine which regards the transcendent as purely impersonal and *Nirvāṇa* as a mere state.

---

[33] *Ibid.*, pp. 70 and 71.   [34] Christmas Humphreys, *Buddhism* (Penguin Books, 3rd ed., 1962), pp. 78-130. To be precise the Theravāda is the chief sect of the Hīnayāna branch of Buddhism.   [35] Zaehner, *op. cit.*, p. 70, cf. Christmas Humphreys, *op. cit.*, pp. 79 and 85 ff.

Zaehner is almost certainly right, therefore, in classifying the mysticism of Theravāda Buddhism as a form of monistic, as distinct from theistic, mysticism. This difficulty is compounded by the fact that Theravādins repudiate any concept of grace, faith or supernatural help as morally undesirable;[36] that their concept of *Nirvāna* is normally expressed in negative,[37] rather than positive, terms; and that they emphatically do not regard it as, in *any* sense, involving union or communion with another Being. The only possibility of any concept of the love of God, in their case, is on the exceedingly charitable assumption of Charles Davis that all genuine mystical experience (such as some Theravādins seem to enjoy) should be interpreted as God, in his infinite grace, reaching down (as it were) and grasping a human being who is truly reaching up to the transcendent, however mistaken his conception of the nature of the transcendent may be. To put this in his own words:

> My contention is that religious faith precisely as openness to the transcendent in a movement of self-transcendence may, however variously, inadequately or indeed wrongly objectified in doctrines, be interpreted by the Christian as based in reality upon God's immanent presence by grace in men. The grace is a self-gift of God, not by way of objective knowledge, but by a subject-to-subject union. Hence as a reality it may underlie different attempts at objectification. I do not mean that everyone who externally professes and practises religion in the various traditions is necessarily open to God's grace. This is not so among Christians. I mean that the general structure of religious faith is the *locus* of God's grace and when genuine embodies and manifests it.[38]

How this theory can, in Davis' view, be reconciled with the

---

[36] Charles Davis, *op. cit.*, pp. 93 and 94.   [37] Cf. Christmas Humphreys, *op. cit.*, p. 78.   [38] *Ibid.*, pp. 86 f.

Christian conviction that Christ is the only – and, in that sense, the universal – Saviour must be reserved for later chapters in this book. What concerns us now is the very different tenets of the majority of Buddhists and Hindus. For whereas, in Zaehner's words, 'for the non-dualist Vedānta as well as for the Theravādin Buddhists and the Jains, man, in his eternal essence, *is* the greatest spiritual presence in the universe',[39] other Hindus, who reacted against Śankara's rigid monism, insisted that 'the soul's realization of its own timelessness and isolation is not the final purpose of human existence, which is rather that soul's union and communion with God and its re-union with a transfigured body'.[40] Again, in Mahāyāna Buddhism – to quote Davis' exceedingly concise summary of a variety of different doctrines –

> the historical Buddha receded into the background. A religion of worship developed, directed to heavenly Buddhas, notably Amitabha, and to various great Bodhisattvas.[41] These Buddhas and Bodhisattvas became saviours, who prepared a Pure Land[42] or paradise for their faithful, where conditions were more favourable for the attainment of Nirvāṇa. Hope of reception into the Pure Land of Amitabha took the place for some of Nirvāṇa as a goal. The means of salvation was now the invocation of the heavenly Buddha in faith[43] – as, for example, in the hymn
>
> Have ye faith in Amita's Vow
> Which takes us in eternally,

---

[39] *The Concise Encyclopedia of Living Faiths* (London, Hutchinson, 2nd ed., 1977), p. 409.   [40] *Ibid.*, p. 413.   [41] Beings of Enlightenment who defer their own final deliverance from the world in order to save other people. Cf. Christmas Humphreys, *op. cit.*, pp. 158 ff.   [42] Pure Land Buddhism is today widespread in Japan and was so, previously (at least), in China. Amitabha, or Amida (a Bodhisattva who has now become a heavenly Buddha) is their special 'saviour'.   [43] *Op. cit.*, p. 106. Cf. Christmas Humphreys, *op. cit.*, pp. 161 ff.

> Because of Him, of his Great Grace
> The Light Superb will all be thine.[44]

Another widespread variety of Buddhism today, particularly in the West, is Zen-Buddhism. This is closer to Theravāda than to Mahāyāna Buddhist doctrines in most respects, but differs sharply from the former in 'positing an enlightenment or intuitive grasp of the truth not only at the end of the Path but here and now as they persevere in the Path itself'.[45] To attain this Zen-Buddhists must meticulously follow a special system of posture, breathing and meditation, very similar to the Hindu Yoga regime. Thervādins, by contrast, put their main emphasis on a knowledge of the 'Four Aryan Truths' — that human existence necessarily involves suffering or 'Anguish' (*dukkha*); that the source of suffering, or the 'Arising of Anguish', is our attachment to existence, possessions, etc., which amounts to a positive craving (*tanhā*); and that the only escape, or the 'Stopping of Anguish', is first by resolving to have done with all such craving for, and attachment to, the transient, and then by practising the eightfold discipline, moral and mental, of the 'Middle Way' as the path to *Nirvāṇa*. But they teach that this is seldom, if ever, reached until after an indefinite number of re-births — although this doctrine is much more difficult to understand in Buddhism than in Hinduism, for Buddhists (unlike Hindus) deny that there is any eternal 'soul' to be re-incarnated. What they believe is that desire (*tanhā*), if not eliminated, generates another being which inherits the *karma* of the person who has died[46] — and even that it is possible for this new being, in certain states of mind, to remember, in part, his former existences.

---

[44] H. D. Lewis and R. L. Slater, *World Religions* (C. A. Watts, 1966), p. 18 — quoting *The Shinshu Seiten: The Holy Scriptures of Shinzu* (The Houpa Hongwanji Mission of Hawaii, 1955), p. 236.   [45] *Ibid.*, p. 76.
[46] Cf. Charles Eliot, *Hinduism and Buddhism* (Edward Arnold, 1921), Vol. I., pp. 191-98.

At first sight it would seem that Theravāda and Mahāyāna Buddhism, in its various forms, represent almost totally different religions – as might also, in part, be said of various forms of Hinduism. But Charles Davis has emphasized the role that the *Sangha*,[47] or monastic order, has played in keeping a link between the two by the prominence it has given to the 'contemplative ideal'. So

> Philosophically a synthesis of the divergent elements was achieved in the Three-Body doctrine. There are three bodies or aspects of the Buddha. There is the transformation-body at the human level. The various heavenly Buddhas are manifestations of the Buddha in his enjoyment-body or body of spiritual bliss. At the deepest level there is the *dharmakaya*, the body of *dharma* or truth, essence, being. At that level Buddha means the impersonal, undifferentiated Absolute or Ultimate; the second or heavenly level consists of personal, differentiated forms of the Buddha-essence; the third level is the earthly manifestation of these. In that philosophical form Mahāyāna Buddhism is similar in structure to Advaita Vedānta.[48]

We have already referred, in passing, to the theological problem – tackled by Charles Davis in *Christ and the World Religions* – as to what reconciliation, if any, can be found between the tenets of these 'Eastern', 'Indian' or 'immanentist' religions and the exclusive position accorded to Jesus Christ by the New Testament and orthodox Christianity all down the centuries. His suggestion is that in every religion there is 'a thrust towards and a response to the transcendent', however this may be conceived. And he argues that:

> in each concrete mode there is a seeking of that which lies beyond the transitory world of everyday experience

---

[47] Often spelt *Saṃgha*.   [48] *Op. cit.*, pp. 106 f. For a further treatment of Buddhist doctrines, cf. pp. 140-155 below.

> and is the true reality or the really real. Moreover, whatever may be the different views concerning the role of self-effort as opposed to help from outside in attaining the transcendent, for no religious person is the transcendent of man's making, so that for all the goal is . . . a response to the transcendent that already is. In other words, whatever the necessity of self-effort, the transcendent has to lay hold of or break in upon the seeker.[49]

This may, perhaps, be conceded. Davis himself insists, moreover, that 'faith in Christ implies granting him a universal and final role in regard to human existence and human history. Whatever interpretation is given of the atonement, it cannot fail to regard Christ as having a representative role for mankind'.[50] How, precisely, we are intended to understand this statement is far from clear; but we can certainly agree that the benefits of the atonement are not confined to those who profess and call themselves Christians.

The major emphasis that seems to me to be lacking in Davis' analysis is any insistence that the man who is to partake of God's grace must — surely — have *some* sense of his moral guilt, or at least of his personal inadequacy, and of his need for divine mercy, forgiveness or 'salvation'. I have argued elsewhere that this does not mean that he must necessarily *understand* the atonement, or even know anything about it.[51] After all, the ordinary Israelite who, conscious of his sin and trusting in the divine forgiveness, brought the prescribed animal sacrifice (or, in those offences for which no sacrifice was prescribed, simply threw himself on the grace of God), must have experienced forgiveness on the basis of the timeless efficacy of what God himself did in Christ in his atoning death and victorious

---

[49] *Op. cit.*, p. 86.   [50] *Op. cit.*, pp 127 and 130.   [51] *Christianity and Comparative Religion* (Tyndale Press, 1970), last chapter.

resurrection.[52] But though *knowledge* of this atonement, which was still in the future, was clearly denied him, there must surely have been some God-inspired plea for forgiveness, some real abandonment of himself to the divine mercy. And it is difficult, to say the least, to find any element of this in the attitude commonly taken up by the Advaita-Vedānta or Theravāda mystics — or, indeed, in Jainism, Confucianism, or many of the different schools of thought in Hinduism or Buddhism. Instead, one is reminded at times of the poet's proud assertion 'I am the master of my fate, I am the captain of my soul'. But the Holy Spirit is not bound by conventional doctrines or traditional stances, and under his supernatural influence individual men and women may always be brought to an attitude of heart that puts them within the scope of those passages of Scripture which affirm that he who seeks will find, and that to him who knocks 'it shall be opened'. The basic question is, I suppose, what the individual mystic is, in fact, seeking; and one longs to hear some echo of the tax-collector's prayer, 'God be merciful to me, a sinner'.

I myself have little confidence, I must confess, in the argument that those who deny the existence of God are often wholly without blame, since this seems to be in direct contradiction to St Paul's positive assertion about those who 'suppress' the truth regarding God's 'eternal power and divine nature' which he has, in some measure, 'made plain to them' in his visible acts of creation;[53] about an intuitive knowledge of God which they ignore in favour either of their own philosophy or their idolatrous practices;[54] and about a consciousness of sin which comes from the fact that the good they sometimes do makes them 'a law for themselves' and shows that the 'requirements of God's law are written on their hearts.[55] It is true that men often sin in ignorance; but

[52] Cf. Romans 3:25 and Hebrews 9:15.   [53] Romans 1:18 ff.
[54] Romans 1:21 ff.   [55] Romans 2:14 f. (together with 1:32).

it is also true that they frequently know perfectly well that what they are doing, or the attitude they are taking up, is wrong. We too easily forget that the Johannine statement that 'The true light that gives light to every man was coming into the world' is not only a tribute to the 'Light of the world' but also a condemnation of those who turn away from such rays of that light as have, in fact, partially enlightened the darkness which otherwise surrounds them. It is also relevant to remember St Paul's testimony about Israel as a nation that

> they are zealous for God, but their zeal is not based on knowledge. Since they disregarded (or 'ignored') the righteousness that comes from God and sought to establish their own, they did not submit to God's righteousness —

a testimony from which we *must*, I think, conclude that his 'heart's desire and prayer to God' for them was that they would, indeed, submit to the Christ who 'is the end of the law' and in whom those who believe find the righteousness which is nowhere else available.[56]

But we must return to the concept of the law of God. It is certainly true, as I have in part tried to show, that in the great religions of the East, with all their diversity, there is a basic belief in some sort of transcendental law — whether this is conceived as derived from divine revelation, inherent in the very nature of things, or embedded in immemorial customs. Precisely the same is true, in a rather more primitive form, of the 'tribal' religions of Africa, the Americas, and elsewhere. The outstanding examples of religions which postulate a law which is divinely revealed — directly and in detail — are, or course, Judaism and Islam, which I shall discuss in succeeding chapters. But in Europe the concept of a transcendental law largely took the form of the doctrine of 'Natural Law', or a 'Law of Nature', which

---

[56] Romans 10:1-3 (together with 3:19 f.).

seems first to have appeared among the Greeks, where it can be found as early as Heraclitus of Ephesus. His famous dictum that 'all things flow, nothing abides', led him to the conclusion that

> Wisdom is the foremost virtue, and wisdom consists in . . . lending an ear to nature and acting according to her. . . . They who would speak with intelligence must hold fast to the (wisdom that is) common to all, as a city holds fast to its law, and even more strongly. For all human laws are fed by one divine law.[57]

Thus Heraclitus, a staunch conservative, sought in a transcendental law the ethical foundation for human or 'positive' law. Soon, however, the Sophists used the same doctrine for radical and even revolutionary purposes, for they emphasized the discrepancies between the positive laws of the Greek city-states and that basic moral law which alone has any intrinsic authority, and were the first to propound what came to be regarded as the natural rights of man.

The Sophists' sceptical views were handed on to, and developed by, the Epicureans. But the conservative stance of Heraclitus was elaborated by philosophers such as Socrates, Plato and Aristotle and transmitted to the Stoics, whose attitude may be summarized in the oratorical statement of Cicero that 'True law is right reason in agreement with nature' which 'summons to duty by its commands and averts from wrongdoing by its prohibitions'. So

> one eternal and unchangeable law will be valid for all nations and all times, and there will be one master and ruler, that is, God, over us all, for he is the author of this law, its promulgator, and its enforcing judge.[58]

[57] Fragments 112-14 in Charles M. Bakewell, *Source Book in Ancient Philosophy* (New York: Charles Scribner's Sons, 1907), p. 34 – quoted in H. A. Rommen, *The Natural Law* (trans. T. R. Hanley, B. Herder Book Co., St Louis and London, Fourth Printing, 1955), p. 6.   [58] *The Republic III*, xxii, p. 33 (trans. C. W. Keynes).

It was this concept of natural law which was taken over, and re-interpreted, by the Christian Church. To Thomas Aquinas, for example, this was not only what was contained in the Bible; but, more specifically, the 'eternal law' as this can be apprehended by rational creatures. In principle, therefore, it is accessible to unaided human reason, although St Thomas himself believed that 'the light of natural reason, by which we discern good from evil', is in fact 'the impression of the divine light in us'.[59] In the Reformed theology, with its insistent emphasis on the depravity of human nature since the Fall, on the other hand, the place accorded to natural reason by the Schoolmen was taken, in part at least, by the doctrine of 'common grace' — for the concept of the requirements of a divine law which are written on men's hearts is, as we have seen, clearly Pauline. But in England the influence of Hooker tended to preserve the doctrine of the Schoolmen, for he taught that man always had knowledge of 'Law Rational', which embraces

> all those things which men by the light of their natural understanding evidently know (or at leastwise may know) to be seeming or unbeseeming, virtuous or vicious, good or evil for them to do.[60]

It is worth noting, in passing, that there was almost exactly the same difference of opinion between the Schoolmen themselves as to the *source* of the Law of God as we shall find, in a later chapter, to have existed among Muslim lawyers. Thus H. A. Rommen[61] says that, for Duns Scotus, 'morality depends on the will of God. A thing is good not because it corresponds to the nature of God, or, analogically, to the nature of man, but because God so wills'; and,

[59] *Summa Theologica*, as quoted by d'Entrèves, *Natural Law*, pp. 39-43.
[60] N. Sykes, in *Social and Political Ideas of the Sixteenth and Seventeenth Centuries* (London, 1926), p. 73. For this section of this chapter see my *Liberty, Law and Justice* (Stevens, London, 1978), pp. 15 ff.
[61] *The Natural Law*, pp. 58 f.

for William of Occam, that 'the natural moral law is positive law, divine will. An action is not good because of its suitableness to the essential nature of man . . . but because God so wills. God's will could also have willed and decreed the precise opposite. . . . Thus, too, sin no longer contains any intrinsic element of immorality . . . it is an external offence against the will of God'. But this attitude is in sharp contrast with that of other Schoolmen, including Thomas Aquinas, who found the basis for natural law not *primarily* in the will of God but in his divine essence and reason; and thence also in the nature and reason of man.

Now it is true that the doctrine of Natural Law in its extreme form – that is, that it is possible to derive the principles of a comparatively comprehensive legal system by rational deduction from natural phenomena – is largely discredited today. From one point of view we have not got a sufficiently static or reverential view of natural phenomena, many of which can now be manipulated, for better or for worse, by genetic engineering or other human skills, while from another we have come to see how speculative and subjective such sweeping deductions must be. Among lawyers, for example, those who favour a system of jurisprudence based on natural law are, today, comparatively rare. Yet even in the sceptical West, as I wrote recently,

the concept of natural law will not lie down and die, without survival and without progeny. In countries and periods in which the Rule of Law substantially prevails, it is true, the population at large, and the legal profession in particular, may be content to think almost exclusively in terms of positive law; but, so soon as a dictator comes to power and a regime of tyranny prevails, men's minds turn wistfully once more to some transcendental concept of law and justice by reference to which obnoxious decrees, enactments and judge-

ments can be tested and assessed. This phenomenon
may be aptly illustrated by the situation which obtained in Germany before, under and after the Nazi
regime. Before the advent of Hitler, German lawyers
were in the vanguard of those 'positive' jurists who
insisted that the validity of any law must be judged by
purely objective and legal, rather than subjective and
moral, criteria. But under Hitler there was a palpable
change of heart, since it soon became apparent that
this view played all too easily into the hands of
tyranny . . .[62]

But how can this 'transcendental law' best be described?
Instead of speaking about natural law, a strong case can be
made out for an appeal to what has aptly been called 'creation ordinances', or those 'divinely given structures which
are a part of God's creation'.[63] Thus Dr Oliver Barclay
argues persuasively for

what may be called *creation* ethics as opposed to
natural law. Natural law has to start with experience — what is — and to try to get from there to what
ought to be. This almost always commits the 'natural-
istic fallacy' (*i.e.* it is; therefore it ought to be). . . .
Natural law starts with the world and tries to work to
moral imperatives. Creation ethics start with God and
his revelation and, looking at the world as his creation,
works towards moral imperatives that are both divine
commands and also good sense.[64]

When, moreover, 'moral imperatives' are based either on
'divine revelation' or the 'ordinances and structures' of creation, they are clearly indistinguishable from the Law of
God.

[62] *Op. cit.*, pp. 16 f.   [63] Oliver Barclay, 'The nature of Christian
morality', in *Law, Morality and the Bible* (ed. B. N. Kaye and
G. J. Wenham, Inter-Varsity Press, Leicester, 1978), p. 133.
[64] *Ibid.*, p. 129.

Today, however, we live in a largely secular society. So it is interesting to see the permutations through which the medieval doctrine of Natural Law has in fact passed. First, Grotius himself put forward, as a theoretical assumption, the thesis that the doctrine of a Law of Nature would still be viable and convincing even if there were no God, or if the affairs of men were no concern to him; and to many of his successors this was much more than a mere hypothesis. The result was that there was a partial (although largely unconscious) return to the view of the Sophists to which reference has already been made; and the basic concept underwent a metamorphosis from an emphasis on natural law to an insistence on natural rights; from an appeal to a divine law which man, as a rational creature, could in part discern and apply, to a proclamation of the inherent and 'sacred' rights of man — as in the Virginian Declaration of Rights and the American Declaration of Independence, 1776, and the Declaration of the French National Assembly, 1789. Meanwhile, in what was then the British Empire, the doctrine of natural law was whittled down to the twin concepts of 'natural justice', on the one hand, and 'justice, equity and good conscience' (or its equivalents), on the other. More recently, however, the concept of the 'natural rights of man' has burst upon the world with renewed vigour in the form of the 'Human Rights movement' — which has given birth to a vast proliferation of Declarations, Covenants and Conventions, both national and international, during the last three decades.[65]

In point of fact the 'rights' covered by this documentation represent a very varied and disparate collection. Some are such as we tend to regard as basic to civilized life — such as the right to life, liberty, freedom of conscience, religion, and

---

[65] I have developed this whole subject much more fully in my Hamlyn Lectures for 1976, *Liberty, Law and Justice* (Sweet and Maxwell, London), pp. 15 ff. and 34 ff.

speech; equality before the law; and the essentials of fundamental human dignity (e.g. freedom from torture and from cruel or degrading punishments) – together with a minimum of provisos, where necessary, which are themselves adequately defined. Others are of quite a different nature and are concerned with equality of opportunity and reward, adequate pay, and even provisions for minimum holidays, etc. Now it may, of course, plausibly be argued that all these things are highly desirable, and even that those 'fundamental' rights which have long been recognized cannot really be secured to, or enjoyed by, those who are deprived of the means of livelihood or of access to education. But it is exceedingly difficult to define or enforce some of these economic and social 'rights' – and there is, I think, much to be said for the pattern adopted by the Indian Constitution which devotes Part III to 'Fundamental Rights', which are already fully justiciable before the courts, and Part IV to 'Directive Principles', which represent objectives which the Government is pledged to seek to promote, but which in the meantime are not actionable *per se.*

But the 'Human Rights' movement – even more, perhaps, than the earlier emphasis, at the time of the American and French revolutions, on the 'natural, sacred and inalienable rights of man' – is essentially secular in its inspiration. What bearing, then, can it be said to have on the subject of this book: namely, the Law of God and the Love of God? It relates to our subject, I think, in two ways. First, any discussion of 'rights' presupposes some law, person, legislature or constitution which bestows them. But the recent Declarations, Covenants and Conventions on this subject do not – in general at least – claim to bestow *new* rights, but rather to declare and define rights which already, in principle, exist, and which are even declared to be 'natural' and 'inalienable'. So it is clear that the whole concept can in fact be traced back – however little many of those who champion it today may realize or relish this — to the doctrine of Natural Law, or to the moral law, structure and ordinances of creation. It is man created 'in the image and likeness of God' who may be said to have these 'rights' *vis-à-vis* his fellow men (although the Bible, in point of fact, puts an almost exclusive emphasis on our duties to others rather than the rights we ourselves may claim). In that sense, then, they represent a secular, and largely unconscious, adumbration of the Law of God for his creatures. Secondly, inasmuch as God's Law reflects God's own character, precepts which are designed to promote the fundamental principles of justice and loving concern for others must necessarily testify to the Love of the Supreme Lawgiver which prompts and underlies his Law.

CHAPTER II

The Law of God and
the Love of God in Judaism[1]

I remarked in my last chapter that the outstanding examples in history of religions which have given an absolutely central place to what they accept as literally the 'Law of God' are Judaism and Islam – and it is to them that I now turn. There is, indeed, a marked similarity between the way in which the Law was developed in the two religions. In both there was, initially, a hard core (so to speak) of law which they believed to have been divinely revealed through what was virtually a form of literal dictation: the law given to Moses on Sinai through the mediation of angels,[2] and the revelations vouchsafed to Muḥammad, over a period of years, through the Archangel Gabriel. In both cases, moreover, this came to be supplemented by an equally important corpus of oral law, preserved by the Rabbis and *'ulamā'* respectively, which was regarded as inspired in its content, if not in its actual wording – together with a vast collection of analogical and interpretative deductions, which were treated as authoritative in varying degrees. There can be no doubt, moreover, that

[1] I use this term, unless suitably qualified, to cover the whole period between the time of Moses and the present day – rather than the more limited connotation that is often given to it.   [2] Jubilees 1:27 ff. and 2:1 ff.; Midrash on Psalm 68, para. 10; Exodus Rabbah 29:2. Cf. also Acts 7:53; Galatians 3:19; Hebrews 2:2.

the development of Islamic law itself, in the earliest period, owed a considerable debt to the teaching and methodology of the Rabbis – as, indeed, did both Jewish and Muslim scholars to those principles of Roman law with which they were inevitably familiar through the medium of popular Hellenistic schools of rhetoric.[3] But there were also many differences, of course, between the two religions in their attitude to the law of God – and, still more, to the love of God.

I think it would be true to say that the idea that most Christians have of Jewish law is derived from the New Testament, where the impression we get of the 'teachers of the law and Pharisees' is far from flattering. We find there an understandable emphasis on their rigid legalism; on the way in which they (and their ancestors) had broken 'the command of God' and nullified his word in favour of 'rules taught by men';[4] on the vast proliferation of regulations they had thus compiled and 'put on men's shoulders', but would not themselves 'lift a finger to move';[5] and on their carping criticism of one whom they regarded as an upstart teacher who gave voice to unorthodoxies with an authority they deeply resented. It is clear, moreover, that Jesus himself, while wonderfully gentle with the weak and fallen, was prepared to denounce religious hypocrisy, wherever he found it, in the most scathing terms – and that he found many examples of such hyprocrisy among the contemporary teachers of the law. But it is also important to realize that

> Pharisaism is not to be viewed as one solidly uniform section of Jewry. The Talmud knows six unpleasant types of Pharisee and one type dear to God, men who serve him out of love. Wholesale condemnation of the Pharisees has found its way into dictionaries and

[3] Joseph Schacht, *Introduction to Islamic Law* (Oxford, Clarendon Press, 1964), p. 30.   [4] Matt. 15:3-9.   [5] Matt. 23:4.

popular language, but is not warranted even on the strength of the Gospel records, and Jews of all sections rightly resent it. There are, in fact, passages in the New Testament[6] which show a different type of Pharisee, one who is patient and understanding.[7]

What is true about the whole group is that they separated themselves from all others (hence their name, which is derived from *Perushim*, 'the Separated') to devote themselves to the strictest observance of the Law, which they saw as the only hope of survival, and that it was largely because of their teaching that Paul came to the heart-breaking conclusion that the people of Israel, as a whole, were so set on 'establishing' their own self-righteousness by a meticulous observance of all the minutiae of the law — or, on another view,[8] on relying on that status of national or racial privilege (bestowed on their whole race, they believed, by God's covenant of grace) which they manifested and maintained as their birth-right by their fidelity to that same law — that they were predisposed to refuse to 'submit' to the way of salvation which God had always intended both for Israel and for all men.

But there are a number of misunderstandings to which this picture, if taken in isolation, may easily give rise. One of these is the danger into which extreme 'Dispensationalists' have all too often fallen: namely, that the people of Israel (at least from the time of the promulgation of the law of Moses) were 'under the law' and *not* 'under grace', whereas Christians are now under grace alone. This is a subject to which we shall have to return later; but I must observe in this context that it represents a grave misunderstanding of the Old Testament as well as the New. For not only was it impossible for the Mosaic law to annul the covenant of grace given, many years before, to Abraham, but it is clear that

[6] Cf. Acts 5:38 f and 23:9.   [7] H. D. Leuner, chapter on 'Judaism', in *The World's Religions* (ed. J. N. D. Anderson, Inter-Varsity Press, London, fourth ed., 1975), p. 54.   [8] Cf. pp. 110 f. and 178 below.

the law revealed on Mount Sinai followed, rather than preceded, the redemption of the children of Israel from their bondage in Egypt.[9] So the law of Moses was in fact given to a redeemed people as a way of life, not to an unredeemed people as the means of redemption.

In point of fact a good deal of scholarly work has been done, in recent years, on the form and substance of the Old Testament covenants – and it seems that they substantially follow, with certain significant differences, the broad pattern of secular grants, covenants and treaties which were customary in the ancient Near East. Thus the covenants with Abraham and David, which essentially consist of divine promises and in which the obligations of David or Abraham receive only very brief mention,

> are modelled on royal grants of land and dynasty. As a reward for faithful service great kings used to present vassals or leading officials with land, or in the case of vassal kings with land and dynasty. Much of the biblical terminology reflects the usage of these royal grants. The biblical texts make it abundantly clear, however, that it was divine grace, not human merit, that prompted these covenants and their promises.

By contrast, the Sinaitic covenant

> is not modelled on a royal grant but on a vassal treaty, a legal form in which the vassal's obligations are much more prominent. But even here the laws are set in a context of a gracious, divine initiative. . . . Exodus presents the release from Egyptian slavery and the Sinai covenant as God fulfilling his promise to the patriarchs that he would give the land of Canaan to their descendents (Ex. 2:24-3:17). Half-way between

[9] Cf., in this context, Walter Eichrodt, *Theology of the Old Testament* (trans. J. A. Baker, SCM Press, London, fifth ed., 1964), pp. 280 ff., and *passim*.

Egypt and Canaan the Sinai covenant is concluded. It
begins with a reminder of what God has done thus far:
'You have seen what I did to the Egyptians, and how
I . . . brought you to myself' (Ex. 19:4). Israel's obligations are then alluded to: 'Now therefore, if you will
obey my voice and keep my covenant. . . .' Then finally
a promise is added: 'You shall be my own possession
among all peoples' (Ex. 19:5).[10]

Similarly, the book of Deuteronomy may be said to be 'per-
vaded by this notion of grace and law'. In both the Sinaitic
and the Deuteronomic covenants, law 'is the gift of a
gracious, saving God', whose will it is that, through
obedience to his law, his people should experience more of
his grace.[11]

The secular model on which these covenants were based
was commonly followed, in the Hittite empire, when a 'great
King' conquered a minor King but allowed him to continue
in power. Dr Gordon Wenham believes that in these
covenants the 'Old Testament uses the analogy of God as
"great king" quite deliberately, just as it draws on other
realms of human activity such as the family'. Such treaties
commonly conformed to a stereotyped pattern and used
conventional terms. They started, for example, with the
titles of the great king and an emphasis on the mercy and
kindness he had shown to his vassal. Next, there was a
section which specified the duties owed by the vassal to his
suzerain in fidelity, military support, tribute, etc.; and they
were concluded by an invitation to the gods to witness what

---

[10] Gordon Wenham, in *Law, Morality and the Bible* (ed. by B. N. Kaye
and G. J. Wenham, Inter-Varsity Press, 1978), pp. 4 f. Cf. M. Weinfield,
'The Covenant of Grace in the Old Testament and in the Ancient Near
East', in *Journal of the American Oriental Society*, 90, 1970, pp. 184-203,
and 'Covenant, Davidic', in *The Interpreter's Dictionary of the Bible*,
Supplementary Volume (Abingdon, New York, 1977), pp. 188-192.
[11] *Ibid.*, pp. 6 f.

had been agreed, and an invocation of blessings on those who fulfilled their obligations and curses on those who did not. And this pattern – with the solitary exception of the appeal to pagan gods – is largely reproduced in Exodus and Deuteronomy.

There are a number of consequences – direct and indirect – of the fact that the Mosaic law is framed in this way. For it follows, on the one hand, that these laws are 'more than an abstract system of morality' and take the form of the personal demands of a sovereign God on his covenant people; and it equally follows, on the other, that the Mosaic law differs from most ancient codes in the fact that it is not exclusively made up of case law, with a list of the appropriate penalties for specified actions, but also includes general prohibitions and numerous religious regulations. At the very heart of the covenant is, of course, the command that Israel should love the Lord their God with all their hearts, and that they should have no other gods than him. A further consequence of the personal nature of the relationship between God and his people was that the injunctions that they should be just, merciful and holy were based on the fact that this was true of God himself.[12] And this, in its turn, means that the law represents a reflection of the character of the law-giver. It is for this reason, among others, that the law, in its moral essence, is unchangeable, and the covenant eternal. Disobedience to it would, indeed, bring punishment and calamity, but it would not annul the covenant as such.

Another danger to which an exclusive dependence on the New Testament strictures on the 'Jews' and the 'teachers of the law' may expose us is – as we have noted in passing – to suppose that all Israelites, or all Pharisees and lawyers for that matter, conformed to the same pattern. Our Lord's greeting to Nathaniel 'Behold, an Israelite indeed, in whom is no guile' should of itself be enough to warn us of this

[12] Wenham, *op. cit.*, pp. 9-14.

danger; and one only has to read Psalm 119 to realize how greatly some Jews loved, treasured and delighted in the Law of their God. This is vividly portrayed in a recent book by Dr Stuart Blanch entitled *The Trumpet in the Morning*,[13] where he writes that:

> to the pious Israelite of an earlier era the law was a joy, not a burden – 'I have had as great delight in the way of thy testimonies as in all manner of riches'. That quotation from Psalm 119 itself reveals the difficulty. The Hebrews had many words for law; we have one, and our word is a singularly inadequate word for what the Hebrews understood to be the gift of God at Sinai. The Books of Moses are more rightly represented as Torah, i.e. the teaching of God.[14] The picture is not so much of a stern judge handing down judgements and imposing fearful penalties as of a father teaching his child how to walk and what to eat and how to avoid danger, introducing him to new truths, opening his eyes to the stately ordering of the universe. 'When Israel was a boy, I loved him; I called my son out of Egypt. It was I who taught Ephraim to walk, I who had taken them in my arms; but they did not know that I harnessed them in leading-strings and led them with bonds of love'.[15]

Dr Blanch goes on to emphasize that the Hebrew prophets, when they rebuked sin and appealed to kings and people to repent and mend their ways, 'were not plucking denunciations and precepts from the sky; they were applying the known Torah of God to flagrant abuses of it that they observed in their society'. Mention of the Torah occurs, he says, no less than 49 times in the prophetic writings. At the

[13] Hodder and Stoughton (London, 1979).   [14] And in this sense the term *Torah* is not only used, as we shall see, to cover the oral law, but also the word of prophecy and probably the wisdom of the wise. It is also used at times as an equivalent of the Old Testament as a whole.   [15] pp. 14 f.

very centre of the Torah, moreover, stood the Decalogue; and it is instructive to note how often the denunciations of the prophets echo those central commandments. The prophets were 'radical exponents' of a legal system the authority of which 'rested upon the assumption that the law was the creation of God and had been committed to his chosen people in the phenomena of fire and thunder and smoke at Sinai'.[16]

But what view are we to take of the Decalogue itself? Writers such as Edward Robertson[17] and Anthony Phillips[18] have suggested that the 'Ten Words' were originally given in a shorter form – a hypothesis with which Dr Blanch is inclined to agree. He also leans to Robertson's conjecture that the law as a whole may be regarded as largely originating in a sort of commentary on, and expansion of, the Decalogue. But he has – rightly, in my view – rejected the thesis of Anthony Phillips that the Ten Commandments all represent *criminal* law.[19] It is exceedingly dangerous to attempt to make any sharp distinction between 'criminal' and 'civil' provisions in ancient law, for this was not the way in which people thought in antiquity. In point of fact it is almost impossible to make this distinction with any confidence in Islamic law, roughly a millenium later. No lawyer, moreover, could regard the Tenth Commandment as criminal – unless, of course, one makes the wholly unsubstantiated conjecture of Brevard Childs that 'the original command was directed to that desire which included, of course, those intrigues which led to acquiring the coveted object'[20] (by which, I presume, he means what a lawyer would term conspiracy). But I think Dr Blanch is almost certainly right in

[16] *Op. cit.*, pp. 24-29. But cf. also J. Barton, 'Natural Law and Poetic Justice in the Old Testament' (*Journal of Theological Studies*, April, 1979), pp. 1 ff. [17] *The Old Testament Problem* (Manchester University Press, 1950), p. 90. [18] Ancient Israel's Criminal Law (Blackwell, Oxford, 1970), pp. 1, 2, etc. [19] *Op. cit.*, pp. 63 f. and 69 f. [20] *Exodus* (SCM Press, London, 1974), p. 427.

his conclusion that

> these commandments do not conform to any one
> category nor can they be interpreted in a uniform way.
> In that respect, if in that respect alone, they do not
> conform to what most of us understand by a law code.
> All the more reason therefore for believing that there is
> an element of originality about them. . . . The Deca-
> logue is not just 'ancient Israel's criminal law' or just a
> handbook of ethics or a guide to social conduct or the
> standards by which a believer may judge his attitudes.[21]

It is only when he goes on to say that it 'is *sui generis* — a
strange combination of precept and prohibition, of religion
and ethics, of prohibited acts and prohibited intentions' that
I disagree. The Decalogue is indeed unique in several ways;
but it is going too far to say that it is *sui generis* in the
respects to which Dr Blanch refers, since one can find
precisely the same type of 'strange combination' in the
Qur'ān. And this phenomenon can best be explained in the
case of the Torah, I think, in the way Gordon Wenham
suggests:[22] namely, that they represent some of the 'personal
demands' of a sovereign God on his covenant people — both
similar to, and yet different from, the obligations of a vassal
in the typical suzerain treaties of the ancient Middle East.

When we come to examine in more detail the nature of
this 'strange combination of precept and prohibition, of
religion and ethics', we may find it helpful to follow Article
7 of the Thirty-Nine Articles in analysing the Torah in terms
of those precepts and prohibitions which are moral,
ceremonial and 'civil', respectively — however strange this
might have seemed to an Israelite of old.[23] Thus the
'Commandments which are called Moral' represent those
principles of ethical conduct which God revealed to his
covenant people as the pattern and quality of life he had

[21] *Op. cit.*, p. 69 f.   [22] Cf. pp. 45 ff. above.   [23] Cf. pp. 108 f., 179 below.

graciously designed for his human creatures and now demanded of them. But although this pattern, and these precepts, were designed for man's highest happiness and fulfilment, they are such that fallen men and women can never perfectly achieve or observe. So the central element in the ceremonial law – the sacrificial system – was in essence a way of grace, since it provided a means by which those who had failed to keep the moral law could express their repentance for what they had done, or failed to do, and their faith in the forgiveness of their loving, covenant-keeping God – although this part of the law, too, was expressed in legal terms, and coupled with numerous prohibitions which were designed, *inter alia*, to make it clear that sinful man may not stroll, as it were, into the sanctuary, or the divine presence. As for the part of the Torah which Article 7 classifies as 'Civil', this comprises all those precepts and prohibitions of the law – whether civil or criminal – which concern such miscellaneous matters as manslaughter, rape, slavery, divorce, testimony and, indeed, most of those provisions which would be recognized by a modern lawyer as essentially legal. It is remarkable, moreover, how closely this part of the Torah corresponds with other ancient Near Eastern codes – except that the Mosaic legislation, when compared with the Code of Hammurabi, for example, can be seen to treat offences against the person as of greater gravity, and those against property as of proportionately less significance. But, however that may be, these detailed 'civil' precepts often fall far short of the ideal, for they were prescribed, or permitted, for the day to day government and social relations of a nation which, although heirs of the covenant, often lived in a way which differed very little from that which characterized other nations. There were no doubt always some – whether in the time of the judges, the undivided Kingdom, or in Israel and Judah – who 'delighted' in the law of God and earnestly tried to live accordingly, but there were far more who did not.

Inevitably the question arises, then, of when and why the excessively legalistic approach to the Torah, which we find attributed to the Pharisees and 'teachers of the law' in the New Testament, began to develop. To this question there is no easy answer. First, it must be remembered that, from the very beginning, the written law was always accompanied by an oral explanation and application; and there is an almost inevitable tendency for such explanations to grow into traditional law of ever increasing detail and complexity. Secondly, it would be a mistake to think that this rigorously legalistic attitude was characteristic of the whole people, or even of all those who devoted themselves specifically to the study of the Torah; for there were always those who were more rigid, and others who were more liberal in their approach. There can be no doubt, however, that a tendency towards an almost obsessive devotion to, and elaboration of, the details of the law was in large part fostered by the vicissitudes of history.

But before we turn to some of these vicissitudes, it may be well to pause and reflect. What is fundamental to Biblical Judaism — and, indeed, to most of its post-Biblical manifestations — is a profound belief that God is personal, that he cares about man and that he addresses him through his spoken Word. As Professor R. J. Zwi Werblowsky has put it:

> God called man, and all that man had to do — although it may have been quite a lot — was to listen. To listen, however, means to obey. God wanted man, or rather wanted something of man, and in spite of the obvious theological disclaimers it seems as if the purpose was not solely man's own benefit. God at least appeared to be somehow profoundly interested and involved in what would happen to man. To this end he called the ancestor out of Ur of the Chaldees, and his

descendants, by now a small people, out of their bondage in Egypt. He made a solemn oath and covenant
with them and told them what he would give them and
what they were expected to do. Henceforth they were
to walk in the way of the Lord, hearkening to, that is,
obeying his voice. . . . They were covenanted to God in
a special relationship whose validity was everlasting . . . and there was no escape or respite from the required loyalty. Even unfaithfulness could not dissolve
the Covenant; it would only bring judgement. . . .

This basic attitude of *listening* contrasts character-
istically with another attitude, perhaps best portrayed
by Greece, which may be described as *seeing*. Listening
brought the Israelite to his goal – doing the will of
God; seeing brought the Greek to his – knowledge. The
decisive Biblical mode of intercourse with the divine
was audition; for the mystery type of religion it was vision. Seeing-knowing or 'beholding' reality appeals to
reason, hearing-obeying appeals to the will. The
former is more static and consequently looks to eternal
and changeless reality; the latter is thoroughly dynamic
and is directed towards events and the movement of
history.[24]

And almost exactly the same words – with the exception of
the references to Egypt and the special concept of the
Covenant – could have been written about the way in which
Muslims think. But we must not be diverted at this point,
and must return to the history of Israel and Judah.

In 721 BC Assyria captured Samaria, the leading citizens
of the Northern Kingdom were taken into exile, and the
country was re-populated with men of mixed race. Naturally enough, this catastrophe was interpreted by many in
Judah, the Southern Kingdom, as a divine judgement on

[23] *Concise Encyclopedia of Living Faiths*, edited by R. A. Zaehner
(Hutchinson, London, 2nd ed., 1977), pp. 11 and 12.

Israel for their desertion not only of the throne of David but of the sanctuary and law of God. Soon, however, Assyria was itself conquered by Babylon; and although the Kingdom of Judah remained, for nearly one hundred and fifty years after the fall of Israel, faithful to the Davidic monarchy and accorded a somewhat greater (although sadly fitful) allegiance to the law of God, in 597 BC the Babylonians invaded the Southern Kingdom, took many of its chief men into exile, and finally, in 586, stormed Jerusalem, rased it to the ground, and burnt the Temple. So the Jewish people were faced with an agonizing problem. The Davidic monarchy, which was to endure for ever, was apparently at an end, and the Temple worship, founded on the pattern revealed for the Tabernacle in the wilderness, was no longer possible. What, then, was left to God's chosen people? As Dr Blanch puts it:

> There was only one answer immediately to hand. Yes, Jerusalem had been taken, the Ark of the Lord had been lost, the sacrifices had been suspended and the king was no more, but they did have 'the law' — not indeed any longer available on the tablets of stone but by now written on the heart of many an Israelite in a foreign land and in some form constituting part of the sacred writings of the people.[25]

In the captivity therefore — and, indeed, in the sequence of events[26] which resulted in the great majority of the Jews being scattered among peoples of an alien culture in the 'Diaspora' — it was the Torah which came to constitute the identity of the true Israel as the sign of the covenant. Deprived of the worship and animal sacrifices of the Temple, the exiles resorted to places of meeting (synagogues) in which the reading and exposition of the Torah was central. Many of the exiles, it is true, came in course of time to adopt

[25] *Op. cit.*, pp. 81 f.   [26] Especially the Fall of Jerusalem in AD 70 and the collapse in the Bar Kochba revolt in AD 135.

the manners and culture of their non-Jewish neighbours. But others – like Daniel, Shadrach, Meshach and Abednego – remained uncompromizingly loyal to their God, their religion, and the law (both written and oral) which now, more than ever, represented its very essence.

It was, moreover, chiefly people of this type who responded to the call to return to Jerusalem under Ezra and Nehemiah, both of whom did their utmost to bring the 'people of the land' back to a whole-hearted observance of the law in a theocratic society in which the worship of the God of Abraham, Isaac and Jacob displaced the recurrent polytheism of the past. But in the long period of more than five hundred years between the beginning of this very partial return to the 'promised land' in 539 BC and the Christian era, two new factors intervened: first, the Macedonian conquests, followed by the long dominance and pervasive influence of Hellenistic culture, both in Palestine and around the Mediterranean; and, secondly, the military and political ascendancy of Rome. So in Palestine itself, and throughout the many lands in which the considerable majority of the Jewish people continued to live, the battle for national identity continued. In the Diaspora some Jews virtually lost both their faith and their distinctive way of life. Others – like Philo – remained essentially Jewish in their basic allegiance but tried to express and commend their religion in terms of the philosophic thought forms of their Hellenistic compatriots. And yet others retreated, as it were, into a Jewish ghetto and became more and more rigid and introverted.

Somewhat the same polarization, moreover, occurred in Palestine itself. This was the period in which the

varied writings contained in the Hebrew Bible were sifted and settled by the scribes and religious authorities. In those days the so-called 'Men of the

Great Synagogue' (sometimes called the Great Synod), a body of somewhat uncertain composition and duration, applied themselves to the solution of the new spiritual problems which arose with the ever-changing needs of the Jewish people. As recognized authorities on the text and interpretation of the Scriptures, they began to formulate the Oral Law, that part of the divine revelation to Moses which is not recorded in the Five Books of Moses but was transmitted by oral tradition.[27]

There were also those who welcomed Hellenistic culture and the Greek language; and it is noteworthy, in this context, that the majority of the quotations from the Old Testament, even in the New Testament itself, are taken from the Septuagint — a Greek translation completed in Alexandria between the third and second centuries BC. There were those, too, who collaborated with Rome and the puppet Herodian Kingdom. The Essenes, on the other hand, took the diametrically opposite road, which is exemplified, in its most extreme form, in the Qumran community — and it is interesting to note, in this context, that this very 'legalistic' group used to recite, in the 'Community Rule', the words:

> God will draw me near by His grace
> > and by His mercy will He bring my justification.
> He will judge me in the righteousness of His truth
> > and in the greatness of His goodness He will pardon
> > all my sin.[28]

But, besides the Hellenists and the Essenes, there were the Zealots, who may be regarded as the spiritual descendents of the Maccabees[29] in their opposition to the occupying power;

[27] Cf. Leuner, *op. cit.*, p. 52.   [28] Cf. G. Vermes, *The Dead Sea Scrolls* (Pelican Books, 2nd ed., 1975), p. 94. It should, however, be noted that E. Earle Ellis points out that while, at Qumran, justification was by grace alone, it was not, as for Paul, through faith alone. CF. *The Gospel of Luke* (Oliphants, London, 1974), p. 215.   [29] Except, of course, that it was the Seleucids, not the Romans, against whom the Maccabees fought.

the Sadducees, an aristocratic priestly body; and the
Pharisees, to whom reference has already been made. It was
they who 'had the largest following amongst the democratic
urban laity', who 'produced a school of famous Rabbis such
as Hillel and Shammai (who lived just prior to the birth of
Jesus)', who introduced 'those translations of the Scriptures
into the vernacular Aramaic which are known as Targumin
(*from Targum*, i.e. "translation")',[30] and who 'fostered the
establishment of synagogues wherever Jews had settled in the
dispersion of the Mediterranean civilization'.[31]

With the Fall of Jerusalem in AD 70 and the collapse of
the Bar-Kochba revolt in 135, the power of the Sadducees
and the influence of the Essenes and Zealots were broken,
and the Pharisaic interpretation of Judaism prevailed. It was
from the Pharisees that Rabbinic Judaism had first sprung;
and it was under their influence that it increasingly became,
in Zwi Werblowsky's words,

> a religion less concerned with the developing and safe-
> guarding of doctrine than with the formulation of
> norms and rules . . . to relate human action to the
> revealed will of the Creator. The spiritual leaders or
> theologians of Judaism, the Rabbis, are thus essentially
> lawyers. . . . The adage that Judaism is not interested
> in orthodoxy (right faith) but in orthopraxis (right
> action), like most antithetic statements of this kind, is a
> dangerous half-truth. But it clearly brings out the
> main stress of Rabbinic Judaism which could, on oc-
> casion, go to extreme lengths. Thus the strenuous in-
> tellectual labour of *Talmud Torah* (the Study of the
> Law) became the ideal business of life and of supreme
> religious value in itself. The Rabbis seriously debated
> whether study of the Law or performance was to be
> preferred and decided in favour of study. . . . The

[30] More accurately, 'paraphrase' or 'interpretation'.
[31] Cf. Leuner, *op. cit.*, pp. 54 f.

negative side of this development was the hypertrophy of Rabbinic casuistry about legal and ritual minutiae which continued to proliferate as time went on and which often bordered on the absurd. But however absurd in its extremes, any limit set to this development would have been even more absurd and arbitrary. If you are supposed to abstain from work on the Sabbath, then you must also define what constitutes work. Where is the thin line of division between harvesting, reaping and plucking ears of corn? There were thousands of problems of this kind because the whole of life had to be sanctified by being made subject to the Law.[32]

The way in which these problems were solved, and provisions made for new circumstances as they arose, was by means of rules of logic and interpretation (for which, indeed, divine authority was often claimed)[33] which enabled the Rabbis, in Zwi Weblowsky's very charitable words, to 'develop, change and adapt the Law . . . without realizing what they did, or rather in full consciousness of doing nothing but interpreting the Scriptures correctly'.[34] No doubt this was often the case; but sometimes, at least, the result – as in the *ḥiyal* to which Muslim lawyers frequently had recourse[35] – was radically to change the spirit of the law or find a way round an inconvenient command or prohibition.[36] Reference was sometimes made, moreover, to a 'tradition going back to Moses on Sinai' as the basis of the Oral Law which supplemented the written provisions of the Scriptures.[37] And to much of this, as I stated at the

---

[32] *Op. cit.*, pp. 18 f.   [33] Cf. Matthew 23:2 f.   [34] *Ibid.*   [35] Cf. p. 84 below.   [36] Cf. Matt. 15:3-9.   [37] It is significant that the Talmud itself states that 'Whatever a competent student, in the presence of his master, will yet derive from the Law, that was already given to Moses on Mount Sinai' (J. Megillah IV, 74d).

beginning of this chapter, there are partial parallels in Islam.

What may be termed the creative phase of Rabbinic interpretation came to an end somewhat before AD 200, but was followed by a vast proliferation of detailed comments. The results were embodied in the Talmud[38] which comprised the *Mishnah* (at the heart of which is the *Halakhah* collection of authoritative legal teaching and precedents) and the Gemara (or compilation of Rabbinic comments thereon). 'Between them', Leuner says,

> they represent the scholastic activities of the Rabbis from the beginning of the third to the close of the fifth century AD. There is an earlier compilation, the Palestinian Talmud, and a later rescension, the Babylonian. . . . The influence of the Talmud upon Jewish life can hardly be overestimated. It has kept the Jew mentally and theologically alert, it has been his refuge in the long and dreary centuries of persecution and ghetto life when he was debarred from secular studies, and it still exerts considerable influence upon Jewish teaching today, although it is practically unknown to the average Jew. Its vast dimensions can be gauged from the fact that the English translation, edited by Isidore Epstein and published in London between 1935 and 1952, takes up 34 volumes plus an Index volume.[39]

The term Torah comprises the entire body of the written and the oral law, and is the particular treasure of Rabbinic Judaism. It includes no less than 613 commandments, 248 of them positive injunctions and 315 prohibitions. In the words of *The Encyclopedia of the Jewish Religion:*

---

[38] The Palestinian version was completed about AD 375, and the longer Babylonian version at, or shortly after, AD 500.   [39] *Op. cit.*, p. 56.

Unlike wisdom, which is shared by all nations, Torah is the exclusive possession of the Jewish people and shall (Joshua 1:8) not depart from thy mouth, but thou shalt meditate on it day and night.' The Rabbinic passage enumerating those things, the fruit of which man enjoys in this world while the main reward is reserved for the Life to Come, concludes: 'but the study of the Torah is equivalent to them all.' The idea that the Torah is the source of life of the Jewish people is expressed in many Rabbinic parables and homilies, but particularly in the liturgical blessings recited by the person called to the synagogal reading of the Five Books of Moses, and in the daily morning prayer.[40]

Rabbi Hillel, moreover, is reported to have said: 'The more Torah, the more life. . . . He who has acquired for himself words of Torah, has acquired for himself life in the world to come'.[41] So it is easy enough to see what a tendency there was for Jews to regard the study and observance of the Torah as a means of acquiring merit or even earning salvation.

But while the substance of Judaism, with its basic doctrines and detailed legal formulation, was rooted and shaped in the Biblical and Rabbinic periods, its philosophical interpretation, intellectual apologetic and mystical ramifications were largely the work of the Middle Ages. The study of the Bible, the Talmud and the intricacies of legal casuistry continued in much the same way all down the centuries; but the outstanding figures in medieval Judaism grew up in a world in which Greek philosophy had been re-discovered by the Arabs and the thought-forms of their

[40] *The Encyclopedia of the Jewish Religion* (Phoenix House, London, 1967), p. 387.   [41] *Sayings of the Fathers*, II, 8. This quotation (and[(2)] above) were taken from Leuner, *op. cit.*, pp. 56-58.

contemporaries were largely cast in Aristotelian or Neo-Platonic moulds. Man, made in the image of God, was both a rational and moral creature, distinguished from the rest of the animal creation by his power of conceptual thought and his ability to commune with his Creator. It was only natural, therefore, that both reason and mysticism should blossom. As in Islam, once more, certain extremist sects appeared from time to time — such as the Karaite fundamentalists, who refused to accept any authority other than that of Scripture alone. But the dominant figures in eleventh and twelfth century Judaism were Maimonides, Yehuda Halevi and Bahya ibn Pakuda. Maimonides, who was an outstanding Talmudic scholar as well as an illustrious philosopher, believed that the *Torah* was the ideal discipline to lead men to a contemplative knowledge and intellectual love of God. But he was so utterly opposed to anthropomorphism in every shape and form that he rejected any doctrine of the divine attributes which carried the slightest suggestion of corporeality or multiplicity; and he insisted on interpreting every statement about the qualities of the Godhead in a way which reduced them to merely negative assertions. The God to whom he gave his allegiance was emphatically the God of the philosopher rather than the simple believer. Yehuda Halevi, on the other hand, was an outstanding poet whose poetry

> burns with the faithful love of the Community of Israel for its Lord and Redeemer no less than with an intensely personal, mystic love of God and an individual longing for divine communion. . . . Centuries before Pascal, Halevi sharply formulated the difference between the God of Aristotle, who is at best a bloodless abstraction, a 'first cause' or 'prime mover', and the God of Abraham, who is the Living God experienced

in personal relationship and in revelation.[42]

Bahya ibn Pakuda, for his part, was a judge in a Rabbinic
court in Spain; but he was so conscious of the danger of
mere formalism in religion that he set himself to write a
book which represents the first Jewish system of ethics and
expounds an ascetic spirituality which combined the Neo-
Platonic background of contemporary Muslim Ṣūfīs[43] with
Jewish traditional teaching. In his Guide to the Duties of the
Heart, which he wrote in Arabic, he revealed a wide
acquaintance with Muslim as well as Jewish thought and a
profound personal piety and devotion. His debt to both the
Mutakallimīn (the teachers of *Kalām*[44]) and to the *Ikhwān
al-Ṣafā'* is obvious, particularly in his treatment of the Unity
and Attributes of God; in the need for introspection, repentance and asceticism; and in the goal of mystical vision, in
which the soul is capable of 'seeing without eyes, of hearing
without ears, of speaking without tongue, of perceiving
without the sense of perception, and of arriving at conclusions without the methods of reason'. But his insistence
on the study and observance of the Law kept him from
falling into some of the excesses (such as the soul's complete absorption in, and identification with, God) which
some Muslim mystics did not hesitate to teach. Instead, he
emphasized that all wordly desires represent a form of
'secret polytheism'; that any admission of the reality of
'secondary causes' constitutes a denial of man's direct dependence on God alone; and, above all, that our primary
aim should be to have such a love of God as weans the soul
from worldly attractions and makes self-sacrifice for his
sake a positive joy.[45]

In point of fact, mysticism has constituted one element in

[42] Zwi Werblowsky, *op. cit.*, pp. 23 f.   [43] Cf. pp. 97, 103, 122 below.
[44] See pp. 94 f. below.   [45] Cf. *The Jewish Encyclopedia*, vol. II pp.
447-454; Zwi Werblowsky, *op. cit.*, pp. 25 f.

Jewish thought all down the centuries. Even in the Old Testament, for example, we find the legislation of the Pentateuch and the philosophizing of Job and Ecclesiastes side by side with the prophetic visions of Ezekiel and the apocryphal imagery of Daniel; and in post-Biblical times the study of the Torah, devotion to Greek philosophy and mystical yearnings and speculation have all been woven together in the web and woof of Jewish life. The *Merkabah*[46] mystics, for instance, developed a special, ecstatic kind of mysticism which 'taught its initiates ways and means of achieving visionary experiences'. The outstanding feature of this mystical movement was its emphasis on the majestic, the numinous and the awe-inspiring elements in any vision of the divine splendour; and although the esoteric teachings and practices of these *Merkabah* mystics have fallen into oblivion, their influence on Jewish liturgy remains until today.[47]

But much the most widespread and important manifestation of Jewish mysticism was the Ḳabbalah (or 'Cabala'), which was far more exotic in its speculations. The name comes from the Hebrew word Qabbalah, or 'the received or traditional lore', by which the Ḳabbalists meant both Jewish tradition in general and their own esoteric teaching in particular. The name does not occur in literature before the eleventh century, but the Ḳabbalists claimed that their teaching could be traced back to Sinai, where the Lord is said to have commanded Moses: 'These words shalt thou declare, and these shalt thou hide' (IV Esdras 14:5 f); and it certainly owed a debt to the apocalyptic books of the

---

[46] *Merkabah* literally means 'chariot', and stands here for the heavenly Chariot-Throne, with special reference to Ezekiel 1 and 10.
[47] Cf. Zwi Werblowsky, *op. cit.*, p. 26; *The Jewish Encyclopedia*, Vol. VIII, pp. 498 ff.; G. G. Scholem, *Jewish Gnosticism, Merkabah Mysticism and Talmudic Tradition* (The Jewish Theological Seminary of America, New York, 1960).

Apocrypha, to Jewish Gnosticism, to Neo-Platonism, to the
esoteric doctrines in the Talmud, and even Zoroastrian
dualism – and had considerable affinities with the writings
of the Qumran community. The *Sepher-Yezirah* (probably
dating from the seventh or eighth century) testifies to a great
speculative interest in the relation between God and the
world, and posited ten emanations from the Deity called
sefiroth. These are not identical, however, with the ten
sefiroth enumerated in the later Ķabbalah movement,
which appeared, at much the same time but in different
forms, in Germany, Spain and Southern France, with the
Zohar (which can probably be dated early in the fourteenth
century) as its chief text. The basic problem which con-
fronted the Ķabbalists was, in effect, how to link together
two incompatible conceptions of the Deity: the living
dynamic God of the Old Testament and the static abstraction which the philosophers had enthroned in his place.
Starting from the contemporary Jewish teaching which,
under Aristotelian influence, held that the 'attributes' of
God were purely negative, they called him En-Sof, the absolutely Infinite, and proceeded to grapple with the con-
sequential problem regarding the nature and origin of the
universe. In place of the (to them) impossible concepts of the
eternal existence of anything other than the Infinite, on the
one hand, or of his creation of the world *ex nihilo*, on the
other, they thought in terms of divine 'irradiation' through
these *sefiroth* or emanations. Naturally enough, their critics
complained that they were, in effect, substituting a tenfold
God for the Christian Trinity. But while their system was so
extreme, in one sense, as to include an erotic mysticism
within the Godhead, this had no place in man's relationship
with God. Instead, as Zwi Werblowsky puts it, 'the supreme
and central mystery of the Ķabbalah is the Holy Union or
"sacred marriage" between two aspects of the divine or, in
other words, the Unification of God'. The task of the

Kabbalist was to 'promote this end by contemplative efforts and a holy life'. It was for this purpose, indeed, that man had been brought into being, according to the Kabbalistic teaching of Isaac Luria in the sixteenth century, so that man might be God's helper in the struggle to bring about the 'salvation of the world (including matter) by a life of sanctity, concentration and fulfilment of the divine Law which is mystically related to the structure of the cosmos'. This was the special responsibility of Israel. So, instead of man being entirely dependent on God for his own salvation, the Kabbalists taught that God was partially dependent on man in the great work of redemption in which he and man were united, and which was even 'virtually related to the inner life of the Godhead itself'.[48]

This weird system of mystic speculation was the dominant element in Jewish piety from the sixteenth century until it was discredited by outbursts of Messianism and even antinomian excesses. But it was then succeeded by another great mystical movement called Hasidism or 'Chassidism'. This name, which simply means 'the pious ones', was not wholly new, but now came to be applied particularly to a revivalist reaction against Orthodox Judaism which

originated in Poland and the Ukraine in the eighteenth century and spread to other parts of Eastern Europe and then to the United States and Israel. After being long connected with the poorer, uneducated mass of Eastern Jewry, it gradually won respect and admiration among the learned. Here was a direct approach to God, based on personal experience and prayer rather than on dogma and ritual. The founder of

[48] Cf. Zwi Werblowsky, *op. cit.*, pp. 27-31; *The Jewish Encyclopedia*, Vol. III, article on 'Cabala', pp. 456-479; D. C. Steinmetz, article on 'Kabbalah', in *The New International Dictionary of the Christian Church* (ed. J. D. Douglas, Pasternoster Press, Exeter, 1970), p. 560.

Chassidism, Israel Baal Shem-Tov (c. 1700-60), taught that zeal, prayerful devotion and humility were more acceptable to God than intellectualism.[49] Many of its ideas are derived from the *Sefer Yezirah*, and it also makes use of the *Zohar*, a mystical commentary on the Pentateuch which, as we have seen, was the best known of the Kabbalistic books. Essentially, however, it is characterized

> by a genuine piety and humility that are the outcome of an intense life of prayer, combined with cheerfulness and great enthusiasm. It has had its moments of ecstasy and wild extremes when thousands were carried away by miracle-working 'holy men', who thrived on superstition. But it can also claim to have produced distinguished writers and scholars. The greatest representative of Chassidism . . . was Martin Buber, at once mystic, theologian, scholar and philosopher.[50]

Orthodox Judaism has always held to the doctrine of verbal inspiration in its most extreme form, at least in so far as the Pentateuch is concerned, and the Torah as a whole is regarded as so absolutely and fully inspired that 'every letter and phrase bears the mark of its divine origin'.[51] Here traditional Jewish teaching has been reinforced by the Hellenistic concept of the divine Logos, which Jews readily identify with the Torah. This is regarded by the orthodox as sharing in the immutability of its divine Author, and thus preserved from all corruption. As a consequence, Higher Criticism of the Pentateuch has been summarily rejected by Orthodox Judaism.[52] But the substantial emancipation of Jewry, over the last two centuries, from most of the discrimination, humiliation and active persecution of the

[49] Leuner, *op. cit.*, pp. 80 f.   [50] *Ibid.*, p. 81.   [51] *Ibid.*, p. 64.
[52] Cf. *The Encyclopedia of the Jewish Religion*, p. 293; Leuner, *op. cit.*, p. 79; Zwi Werblowsky, *op. cit.*, p. 34.

Middle Ages, with their ghettoes, prohibitions and pogroms, has had the effect of making many Jews want to free themselves from their distinctive way of life and assimilate with the patterns of thought and behaviour which prevail amongst most of their fellow citizens in the modern world. The result was the emergence of 'Liberal' and 'Reform' Judaism, both of which were inclined to welcome Biblical criticism as supporting their desire to liberate themselves from the straitjacket of the Torah and substitute a purely ethical Judaism. Thus Dr Claude Montefiori, the leading protagonist of Liberal Judaism in Britain, has stated that this movement

> modifies or enlarges the doctrines of the past so as to make them consistent with each other and in harmony with the highest conceptions of the truth to which it can attain. It deliberately aims at universalism and universalization. It sets out to emphasize the 'prophetic' elements in Judaism, and to minimize or negate the 'priestly' elements. It gives up all praying for the restoration of the Temple and of animal sacrifices. It sets the Prophets above the Law.[53]

In 1926 Liberal and Reform Judaism formed a World Union for Progressive Judaism. 'Conservative' Judaism, on the other hand, falls midway between the Orthodox and the Progressives. It has taken over some of the external modes of worship of Reform Judaism, such as prayers said in the vernacular; but it claims to accept the entire structure of Rabbinic tradition, although it does permit an interpretation of the Law which is 'in accordance with modern needs and convictions'.[54]

In regard to the concept of atonement, on the other hand, it seems that all groups of theologians are agreed, however

---

[53] *The Old Testament and After* (Macmillan, London, 1923), pp. 557 f.; Leuner, *op. cit.*, p. 80.   [54] Leuner, *op. cit.*, p. 79.

widely they may differ on other points. Dr Hertz, for example, insists that:

> the initiative in atonement is with the sinner (Ezekiel 18:3). He cleanses himself on the Day of Atonement by fearless self-examination, open confession, and the resolve not to repeat the transgressions of the past year. When our Heavenly Father sees the abasement of the penitent sinner, He sprinkles, as it were, the clean water of pardon and forgiveness upon him.[55]

Nothing else is needed, for Judaism does not believe in the doctrine of original sin; instead, it emphasizes original virtue and righteousness. Sin began, the Rabbis teach,

> with the disobedience of Adam to the divine commandment, and it has continued historically ever since. The usual view is that men are given a clean sheet at birth, and that if they allow it to become dirty, they are themselves responsible. . . . The principal theory offered is that every person is born with an impulse or inclination towards evil, the *yetzer ha-ra*, which enters into his nature the moment he emerges from the womb. This is more or less equivalent to what the Christian would call the power of temptation. It is, or should be, counterbalanced in the Jew by the good inclination, the *yetzer ha-tobh*. Victory in the struggle is by no means assured, for the enemy is insidiously strong (Genesis 8:21).[56]

Yet Professor M. L. Margolis states in his Credo:

> I believe that man possesses a divine power wherewith he may subdue his evil influences and passions, strive

---

[55] *The Pentateuch and the Haftorahs* (Soncino Press, London, 1938), p. 484. This statement, with its reference to the Day of Atonement, must of course be understood as applying to Israel as a people under the Covenant.   [56] Roy A. Stewart, *Rabbinic Theology* (Oliver and Boyd, Edinburgh, 1960), pp. 76 ff.

to come nearer and nearer the perfection of God and commune with Him in prayer.[57]

Zionism has, in one sense, burst like a bombshell on the Jewish scene. The initial demand was for a homeland and a Jewish State, wherever it might be situated. But this was soon eclipsed by the vision of the 'promised land' and the home of their fathers. This was bound to have an almost mystical appeal to Jews. In another sense, however, little has changed in regard to their religious faith — except that now the Judaism of the Diaspora and 'the Judaism of the home-land' co-exist at the same time. But present-day Israel, in Zwi Werblowsky's words:

> has its orthodox extremists who ignore the ungodly, secular state and refuse their loyalty to it. To them the arrogation of the name 'Israel' by a secular state is sheer blasphemy. On the other hand there is the secularist and nationalist majority, a large percentage of which still has some vague sentimental or purely social attachments to the 'national' religion. There are also the religious Zionists.[58]

This 'ungodly, secular state' has retained the general structure of secular law which existed in Palestine under the British Mandate, and which represented, in point of fact, an extraordinary amalgam of elements derived from several heterogeneous sources. Since then a lot of Israeli legislation has, of course, been promulgated — including a number of 'fundamental laws' which prevail over any other law, what-ever its origin; but it is only in the sphere of family law that Rabbinic Law has been rigorously applied to all Jews. As a result, those who cannot marry under that law have to travel to Cyprus, or elsewhere, to contract a marriage which will

[57] Cf. Leuner, *op. cit.*, pp. 61 f.   [58] *Op. cit.*, pp. 37 f. On the import-ance of 'The Land' for Jews (and Christians), cf. W. D. Davies, *The Gospel and the Land* (University of California Press, Berkley & London, 1974).

then be recognized in Israel under the provisions governing Private International Law. In a *very* few cases means have been found somewhat to mitigate, in practice rather than theory, the impact of Rabbinic Law: for example, ways have been devised by which the courts virtually compel a reluctant husband to pronounce a divorce (which is his exclusive right) in response to the plea of a wife whose marriage has become intolerable. But throughout this book the term 'law' has primarily been used in an ethical or transcendental sense to cover all that is believed to be the revealed will of God, rather than to refer to the law which human courts can, or do, enforce.

To sum up, then, it is clear that the Law of God is fundamental to Judaism. This is symbolized by the *Barmitzvah* ceremony, at which a Jewish boy who reaches the age of thirteen becomes a 'Son of the Commandment'. At this he recites the words: 'Blessed art Thou, O Lord our God, King of the Universe, who hast chosen us from all peoples, and hast given us Thy Torah.'[59] So it is, I think, true to say that Orthodox Judaism has been basically a religion of law, from which the recurrent mystical movements have represented, in part, a reaction in favour of a religion of love. Even so, the *primary* emphasis even in these movements has been on the love man should have for God rather than the inexpressible love of God our Redeemer for his wayward creatures. It would, perhaps, be fair to say that, to most Jews, God is a merciful and benevolent Heavenly Father rather than a God who loves to the uttermost. But it would be a grave mistake to imagine that the Old Testament is all law or in any way devoid of an emphasis on grace; for we have already seen that the Law of God was, originally, only one part of a Covenant of Love, and that this covenant was firmly based on God's unmerited grace.

It is true that it is primarily God's love for his covenant

[59] Cf. Leuner, *op. cit.*, p. 67. Cf. Pirke Aboth III, 18 ff.

people that is emphasized in the Old Testament, as in Deuteronomy 7:7 and 8, where we read: 'The Lord did not set his affection on you and choose you because you were more numerous than other peoples, for you were the fewest of all people. But it was because the Lord loved you and kept the oath he swore to your forefathers that he . . . redeemed you.' Similarly, I Kings 10:9 speaks of the Lord's 'eternal love for Israel'; Isaiah 63:9 declares that in 'his love and mercy he redeemed them'; and Jeremiah 31:3 puts into the mouth of God the affirmation 'I have loved you with an everlasting love; I have drawn you with loving-kindness'. But this is only a small selection of such verses, which recur again and again. Hosea, for example, recounts how the word of the Lord came to him, saying: 'Go, show your love to your wife again, though she is loved by another and is an adulteress. Love her as the Lord loves the Israelites though they turn to other gods';[60] that 'When Israel was a child I loved him. . . . I led them with cords of human kindness, with ties of love';[61] and that, in spite of their unfaithfulness, 'I will heal their waywardness and love them freely'.[62] Similarly, Zephaniah declares: 'The Lord your God is with you, he is mighty to save. He will take delight in you, he will quiet you with his love, he will rejoice over you with singing.'[63]

There are also, however, references in the Old Testament to a love which is not confined to God's covenant people. Thus the divine Wisdom states, in Proverbs 8:17: 'I love those who love me, and those who seek me find me', while Proverbs 15:9 affirms that 'The Lord detests the way of the wicked, but he loves those who pursue righteousness'. More comprehensively, Psalm 33:5 declares: 'The Lord loves righteousness and justice; the earth is full of his unfailing love' (where the Authorized Version translates the last phrase as 'The earth is full of the goodness of the Lord').

[60] Hosea 3:1.   [61] Hosea 11:1-3.   [62] Hosea 14:4   [63] Zephaniah 3:17.

There are, moreover, many references to God's mercy, compassion, pity, kindness, graciousness and tender mercies, etc., where the New International Version sometimes translates the relevant Hebrew word as 'love'. In Psalm 145:9, for example, the NIV states that 'The Lord is gracious and compassionate, slow to anger and rich in love.[64] The Lord is good to all; he has compassion on all he has made'. Similarly, Exodus 34:6 proclaims that the Lord is 'the compassionate and gracious God, slow to anger and abounding in love[65] and faithfulness, maintaining love[66] to thousands, and forgiving wickedness, rebellion and sin', while Jonah complains, when God spares Nineveh, that 'I knew that you are a gracious and compassionate God, slow to anger and abounding in love,[67] a God who relents from sending calamity'.[68] Again, Psalm 116:5 declares that 'The Lord is gracious and righteous, our God is full of compassion'; Psalm 57:10 that 'great is your love,[69] reaching to the heavens, your faithfulness reaches to the skies'; Psalm 86:5 that 'You are kind and forgiving, O Lord, abounding in love[70] to all who call to you'; and Psalm 89:1 and 2 that 'I will sing of the love[71] of the Lord for ever . . . I will declare that your love[72] stands firm for ever, that you established faithfulness in heaven itself'. And similar examples could be multiplied.

It seems, however, that it was only in the post-exilic Jewish community that the concept of a love of God 'that could not possibly stop when physical life ends but would have to continue on the other side'[73] really matured. Some of the Rabbis not only rose above the narrow concept of God's love for Israel alone but revolted against the essentially Hellenistic doctrine of a God who was so transcendent and impassible that he could not really care about the world of men. In

---

[64] AV 'great mercy'.   [65] AV 'goodness'.   [66] AV 'mercy'.
[67] AV 'great kindness'.   [68] Jonah 4:2.   [69] AV 'mercy'.   [70] AV 'mercy'.
[71] AV 'mercies'.   [72] AV 'mercy'.   [73] Leuner, *loc. cit.*, p. 52.

contrast, as Abraham Heschel wrote, 'the God of the prophets is all concern, too merciful to remain aloof to His creation'. There are, indeed,

> two poles of prophetic thinking: the idea that God is one, holy, different and apart from all that exists, and the idea of the inexhaustible concern of God for man, at times brightened by His mercy, at times darkened by His anger. . . . He is the father of all men, not only a judge; He is a lover engaged to His people, not only a King. His love or anger, His mercy or disappointment, is an expression of His profound participation in the history of Israel and all men.[74]

[74] A. J. Heschel, 'The Concept of Man in Jewish Thought', in *The Concept of Man* (ed. by S. Radhakrishnan and P. T. Raju (Allen and Unwin, London, 1960), pp. 124 f. – as quoted by Leuner, *loc. cit.*, p. 53.

CHAPTER 3

The Law of God and
the Love of God in Islam

We must now consider the religion of Islam,[1] which is at
once so similar to, and yet so different from, Judaism. But
before we embark on this study, a question that may well be
uppermost in many people's minds is the degree to which
what has been termed the 'Islamic Revolution' in Iran that
ousted the Shah, and the Revolutionary Council which (as I
write) exercises such control as now exists in that country,
may properly claim to be called 'Islamic'. In point of fact
what happened was basically a popular revolution that over-
threw a powerful, but despotic and morally reprehensible,
regime by means of largely non-violent mass demonstrations
and political strikes. Some of those who took part in this
were distinctly left-wing in their political allegiance, while
others would have opted for a liberal democracy in which
Islam was the established religion; but they were prepared to
unite under the leadership of a religious figure who had
amply demonstrated his bitter and implacable hostility to
the Shah. The vast majority of Iranians are, however, Shī'īs
of the Ithnā 'Asharī persuasion,[2] who habitually accord a

[1] This is the proper term for what is often mis-named 'Mohammadanism'.
It is the verbal noun from the Arabic root *aslama*, meaning to 'surrender'
or 'yield' to the will of God. One who follows this religion should be called
a *Muslim*, which represents the present participle from the same root.
[2] Cf. pp. 81, 85 f., 88 below.

much more exalted position to their religious leaders than
do Sunnī, or 'orthodox', Muslims. These leaders themselves,
moreover, tend to be distinctly introverted and even
medieval in their thinking, while their followers manifest a
marked degree of religious fanaticism. There can be no
doubt, however, that the special courts which condemned so
many to death were primarily revolutionary rather than
'Islamic', and that taking diplomats as hostages is indefens-
ible in Islamic as well as International Law. So we must
return to our objective comparison between Islam and
Judaism.

The Qur'ān certainly resembles the Torah in the fact that
it represents a 'strange combination of precept and prohibition, of religion and ethics' — and, indeed, of history and
much else besides; but the proportion of strictly legal
material is very much smaller. It is believed by orthodox
Muslims to have been written from eternity in Arabic in
heaven, and to have been revealed to Muḥammad in in-
stalments as circumstances demanded — at times, at least,
in something approaching a state of trance — by the Archangel Gabriel, over a period of some twenty years. The word
Qur'ān can be translated either 'reading' or 'recitation', and
it was certainly regarded by Muḥammad as constituting the
divinely inspired book which the Arabs — unlike some of
their neighbours — previously lacked. In the words of Professor Arthur Jeffery:

> It is the source from which the Muslim community
> draws the primary prescriptions for the regulation of
> daily living, and to which its people turn to find
> nourishment for their devotional life. . . . The Qur'ān
> is the word of Allah. Later Muslim piety, it is true, has
> made much of the person of the founder, but it was the
> Book, the Qur'ān, not the person Muḥammad, which
> was the significant factor in forming the mould in

which the Islamic system took shape. . . . The Scripture of no other community, not even the Old Testament among the Jews, has had quite the same
influence on the life of the community as the Qur'ān
has had in Islam.[3]

Unlike many other sacred books, moreover, it

was not the product of the community in the sense that
they decided that this was the collection of writings
which had grown up in the community and in which
they heard the authentic voice of religious authority,
but it was formed by one man and given to the community on *his* authority as a collection of 'revelations'
which was to be regulative for their religious life.[4]

There were, indeed, ample precedents in the ancient
Near East for the belief that men might be the recipients of
divine instructions – whether by means of omens, oracles or
dreams. Sometimes these instructions were even believed to
represent the communication of the contents of some
heavenly tablet; or, again, they might take the form of
Codes of Law which some king claimed to have compiled,
under divine inspiration, 'to restore the Law of God'.[5] It was
thus that

the Jews came to believe that the Torah was in written
form with God long before the creation of the world,
that its prescriptions were in part made known to and
observed by Adam and the Patriarchs before it was
revealed in its fullness by being brought down to
Moses, and that it will be revealed anew when the
Messiah comes.[6]

Professor Jeffery argues, moreover, not only that Muḥammad derived from the Jews (whether in Madina or elsewhere) some such concept of Scripture, but that this
explains references in the Qur'ān to the 'Mother of the

[3] Arthur Jeffery, *The Qur'ān as Scripture* (Russell F. Moore, New York,
1952), pp. 3-5.   [4] *Ibid.*, p. 6.   [5] *Ibid.*, p. 14.   [6] *Ibid.*

Book', to a 'preserved tablet', and to 'the entire Book' – which, it would seem, the Prophet thought of as comprising both the revelations given to previous 'Messengers' and also those vouchsafed to him by Gabriel.[7]

A further example of what I have called 'similarity with a difference' between Judaism and Islam may be found in the Oral Law. The similarity is that in both religions this oral law was accepted as an inspired amplification, and sometimes even amendment, of the written law, while the difference consists in the fact that, in Sunni or 'orthodox' Islam, the oral law was ascribed exclusively to Muḥammad. Thus whereas, in Judaism, the oral law which was ultimately committed to writing in the Talmud emanates from many different authors, and is ascribed to 'Moses' only in the most figurative sense,[8] the *aḥādīth* (or traditions) of Islam which, after a period of oral transmission, came to be included in one or more of six recognized books, all derive their authority from the claim that they represent an account of something which Muḥammad himself did, said, or permitted to be said or done. In other words the normative element in the traditions is the *sunna* or practice of the Prophet which they are alleged to establish. It is true that a few of these traditions, called *aḥādīth qudsiyya*, are accepted as words spoken to Muḥammad by God himself which for some reason have not been incorporated in the Qur'ān; but the authority of the vast majority rests on the belief that *all* that the Prophet of Islam did, said or permitted was divinely inspired in content, although in the *aḥādīth* (in contradistinction to the Qur'ān) this inspiration does not extend to the actual wording.

In point of fact, however, the claim that all those tra-

---

[7] *Ibid.*, pp. 15 ff. [8] Cf. pp. 42, 56, 58 above. I say 'general' and 'figurative' in regard to some specific later interpretations; but that the Jews did in fact believe that an oral as well as a written law was revealed to Moses on Sinai there can be no doubt.

ditions commonly accepted as authentic really go back to
some incident in Muhammad's life is manifestly without
foundation. The word *sunna* originally meant no more
than a custom which had been handed down, while in the
ancient schools of law it became a technical term for their
accepted practice. It was the traditionalists, not the lawyers,
who travelled far and wide to seek out stories about the Prophet, while the lawyers of the ancient schools did not always
regard even an apparently genuine tradition about the
Prophet's practice as necessarily normative. But al-Shāfiʻī,[9]
the 'father of Islamic jurisprudence', took a middle line;
for he sided with the traditionalists in asserting that any
authentic tradition from the Prophet must be accepted as an
authoritative source of law, but insisted on much more
stringent criteria of authenticity than they did. In time,
moreover, this attitude came to be accepted in theory
by all the schools; but it was still simple enough for
them to ignore an alleged tradition which went against their
accepted doctrine and practice by questioning its authenticity or by producing a contrary tradition which, they
maintained, had a greater claim to authority or was
intended to 'abrogate' the tradition of which they dis-
approved.

The fact that al-Bukhārī, in compiling the most famous
of all the collections of traditions (*al-Ṣaḥīḥ*), is said to have
considered some 600,000 and to have accepted little more
than 3,000, shows how many spurious traditions were at that
time in circulation. Every tradition accepted as authentic
now consists of two distinct parts: the *isnād*, or chain of
narrators by which it has been handed down, and the *matn*,
or substance of the incident narrated. But while, in course
of time, the *isnād* came to be subjected to the most minute
scrutiny (*Could* the alleged narrators in fact have received

[9] Born AD 767.

the tradition, the one from the other? Were they men whose probity and memory could be trusted? etc.), this sort of questioning was not extended to the *matn*, which not infrequently provides convincing evidence that the story could not possibly have gone back to Muḥammad. It was obviously easy enough, moreover, for an acceptable *isnād* to be transferred from one tradition to another, or for an alleged tradition which had a gap in its chain of narrators (particularly, of course, in the final link with Muḥammad) to be suitably completed.

But the sources of Islamic law were not restricted to the Qur'ān and *sunna* alone. There is, in fact, an alleged tradition – itself almost certainly spurious – that Muḥammad sent a man named Mu'ādh to act as a judge in the Yemen, and that he asked him on what he would base his judgements. 'On the Book of God', he replied. Muḥammad commended this answer, but asked him what he would do if he found nothing in the Qur'ān to help him. 'Then I would follow the practice of the Prophet of God', he replied; and was again commended. 'But what would you do if you could find nothing in the *sunna* either to guide you?', Muḥammad is then alleged to have asked. 'Why, in that case', Mu'ādh is said to have answered, 'I should follow my own opinion (*ra'y*)' – and Muḥammad is depicted as praising God for giving him such an intelligent emissary. But it is clear that it was not long before Muslims began to feel that an individual opinion about what is right must, of necessity, constitute much too subjective and fallible a source for a law which claims to be firmly based on divine revelation. First, too subjective; so, in place of a general sense of what Islam requires, they insisted on an analogical extension (*qiyās*) of some recognized text to include another situation which could legitimately be held to be covered by the principle which that text enunciated. Secondly, too fallible; so, in place of the opinion of a single individual, even in analogical reasoning, they gave pride of place to a decision about which a consensus (*ijmā‘*) could be claimed, whether in the community as a whole or (much more often) among reputable scholars. As a result, the four major sources of the law, which came to be recognized by all the surviving 'orthodox' schools (the Ḥanafīs, Mālikīs, Shāfi‘īs and Ḥanbalīs) are now the Qur'ān, *sunna, ijmā*[10] and *qiyās*. It is true that the Ḥanafīs sometimes rejected the view to which *qiyās* would naturally lead in favour of an opinion which they considered 'preferable' (and which they said was based on a more subtle form of analogical reasoning), that the Mālikīs did much the same in favour of what they claimed to represent the 'public interest',[11] and that there are certain other secondary sources of the law which have gained partial acceptance; but this need not detain us here.

Two further matters demand mention at this point. First, Islam became divided, at a very early date, in a much more radical way than between schools of law which, however much they differed from each other in comparative details, mutually acknowledged each others' essential orthodoxy. Far the largest of these conflicting groups was made up of those who believed that the fount of direct divine revelation had dried up with the death of Muḥammad, but that the unity and well-being of the Muslim community required that his political – as distinct from his prophetic – authority should be taken over by a succession of 'elected' successors (*khulafā’*, or Caliphs) who could lead it in war and uphold the sacred law (*the Sharī‘a*)[12] in time of peace. The great majority of Muslims who took this view were called Sunnīs,

[10] Which is now accepted chiefly on the basis of an alleged tradition (which was not known, it seems, when al-Shāfi‘ī wrote about *ijmā‘* in *al-Risāla*) that Muḥammad had once said: 'My community will never agree in error.'   [11] These two sources are termed *istiḥsān* and *istiṣlāḥ*, respectively.   [12] This term originally meant the path to a watering place; and then, technically, the path of God's commandments (or the sacred law).

or the 'orthodox' followers of the practice (*sunna*) of the community. But there were two dissident groups. The larger of these, originally called *Shī'at 'Alī*, or the partisans of the fourth Caliph, insisted that God *could* not have left such a vital matter as the leadership of the Muslim people to the vagaries of human election. On the contrary, he had designated 'Alī and his successors as its God-appointed leaders or Imāms, to each of whom, in succession, had been passed an esoteric knowledge of the meaning of the law which was previously vouchsafed only to the Prophet. Soon, however, the Shī'a itself underwent a great deal of fragmentation; and the principal sub-sects which have survived are the Zaydīs, the Ithnā Asharīs (or 'Twelvers') and the Ismā'īlīs.

The Zaydīs, who come chiefly from the Yemen, are the most moderate of the Shī'a, and their law differs little from that of the Sunnis. They believe that any descendent of 'Alī and Fāṭima (who was not only 'Alī's wife but Muḥammad's only surviving child) might establish himself as Imām by reason of his learning and his force of arms. The 'Twelvers', who are also called the Ja'farīs after their sixth Imām (Ja'far al-Ṣādiq), represent the State religion in Iran, more than half the population of Iraq, and scattered communities in India, the Levant and East Africa. They take a much more extreme view of the Imāmate than the Zaydīs, for they regard their Imāms as impeccable and infallible, believing that a divine light-substance passes into each of them by metempsychosis when his predecessor dies; but they also believe that their twelfth Imām 'went into hiding in the will of God' and is now represented by those religious leaders who have attained sufficient learning to be accepted as *mujtahids*.[13] But the most extreme of the Shī'īs — both in their doctrine of the Imāmate and their concentration on *bāṭinī* or esoteric teaching (leading some of the higher initiates into

[13] For this term, see p. 88 below.

a philosophical system very far removed from orthodox
Islam) − are the Ismā'īlīs. They subdivided, many years ago,
into the Eastern Ismā'īlīs or Nizārīs (commonly called the
Khōjas), who regard the Aghā Khān as their living Imām
and as virtually an incarnation of the Deity; and the
Western Ismā'īlīs or Musta'līs (commonly, but somewhat
ambiguously,[14] called the Bohoras) whose twenty-first Imām
went into hiding[15] and is now represented by a plenipoten-
tiary, or Dā'ī Muṭlaq, in each of the further sub-sects into
which they subsequently split. But the other, and quite different, group of Muslims who broke off from the Sunnīs in
early Islam, and were originally termed the Khawārij or
'Seceders', went to the other extreme in their attitude to the
Caliphate. At first they were fierce nomads who regarded all
other Muslims as apostates who should be put to death, and
they constituted a thorn in the side of authority for many
years. Now, however, only the much more moderate Ibāḍīs
of Oman, parts of North Africa, and (until recently) of Zanzibar, survive. These differ little from the Sunnīs in practical
questions of law, and were able − in Zanzibar, at least − to co-
operate with them excellently; but they are still regarded as
'heterodox'.

The second matter that should be noted at this point is
that recent studies have shown conclusively, I think, that the
traditional Muslim view that Islamic law was derived directly from the Qur'ān and *sunna* by a process of pure
deduction, by jurists located in Mecca and Madina, represents a travesty of the facts. It was the customary law of

[14] The point of ambiguity is that the term 'Bohoras' merely means mer-
chants, and that there are Sunnī as well as Ismā'īlī Bohoras. But the term
'Khōjas' is also somewhat ambiguous.   [15] It should be noted, however,
that whereas the hidden Imām of the 'Twelvers', who went into hiding
about 260 AH, is still believed to be alive and will one day reappear to
bring in the Golden Age, the hidden Imāms of the Musta'līs die when
their time comes and are succeeded by their proper successor − so no one
knows who their Imām is at present.

both Arabia and the newly conquered territories, on the one hand, and the administrative practice of the early Caliphs, on the other, that provided the raw material from which Islamic law was quarried, but only after all this had been worked through by Muslim scholar-jurists in the light of certain Qur'anic principles and such traditions as they knew and accepted. By this process they succeeded, at one and the same time, in systematizing and Islamicizing the law — and the priority in this work came from Iraq, not the Hijāz.[16] Strange to say, moreover, the law which was thus developed and applied in the early schools departs, on occasion, from what seems to be the clear teaching of the Qur'ān. In some cases such departures were only temporary, and can be explained easily enough by the difficulty of enforcing some prescription or penalty which was previously unknown to the Arabs. In others it may be said to represent not so much a deliberate departure from a Qur'anic norm as a development, or legal application, of an injunction or prohibition which is expressed in the Qur'ān in embryonic, or purely ethical,[17] terms. But occasionally it represents a clear and long-lasting reversal of Qur'anic teaching, an example of which can be found in the decisive priority which is typically accorded in Islamic law to oral testimony — together with the virtual rejection of documentary evidence — in spite of the detailed instructions in Sūra 2:282 that certain kinds of contracts should be reduced to writing, and how they should be witnessed and proved.[18] It is also relevant to observe in this context that there were, at first, a number of variant versions of the Qur'ān;[19] that it was only under the Caliph 'Abd

---

[16] For this whole subject cf. the magisterial work of Joseph Schacht in *Origins of Muhammadan Jurisprudence* (and elsewhere). [17] As is, indeed, typical of many Qur'anic injunctions. [18] Cf. J. Schacht, *op. cit.*, pp. 224 ff.; and *Introduction to Islamic Law* (Clarendon Press, Oxford, 1964), pp. 10 ff., 18 f., etc. [19] Cf. Arthur Jeffery, *op. cit.*, pp. 3, 89-103; Schacht, *Introduction to Islamic Law*, p. 18.

al-Mālik[20] that these were officially banned and destroyed; and that instances can be found of legal rules based not only on the *textus receptus* but on one of these variants.

Much the same process of selection seems to have taken place in regard to those elements in Islamic law which were almost certainly derived from Roman, Jewish, Byzantine or other foreign sources. It was not that Muslim legal scholars studied other systems of law and deliberately borrowed principles or precepts from them, but rather than Islamic law was wide open to influences of all sorts during the greater part of the first century of the Hijra. Thus the concept of the *ijmā'* of suitably qualified scholars seems to be an echo of the Roman *opinio prudentium*, while the doctrine that 'the child belongs to the marriage bed', the use of legal fictions, etc., can also be traced to Roman law. These were almost certainly brought into Islam by 'the cultured non-Arab converts to Islam who (or whose fathers) had enjoyed a liberal education . . . in Hellenistic rhetoric, which was the normal one in the countries of the Fertile Crescent of the Near East which the Arabs conquered'.[21] Even so, the way in which they were interpreted and applied in the Sharī'a was distinctively Islamic; as may be seen, for example, in the fact that legal fictions were used in Roman law 'to provide the legal framework for new requirements of current practice with the minimum of innovation',[22] while Muslim lawyers resorted to their *ḥiyal* to enable them to achieve some purpose, which seemed to be forbidden by the Sharī'a, without actually transgressing the words of the relevant injunction or prohibition. Recourse to such 'devices' was, moreover, no doubt encouraged by the consideration that there were many provisions in the Sharī'a in regard to which obedience could only be 'blind' (*ta'abbudī*), since no one professed to understand the reason behind them. Examples

[20] 65 AH (AD 685) – 86 (705).   [21] Cf. Schacht, *Introduction*, p. 20. Cf. also pp. 21 and 78 ff.   [22] *Ibid.*, pp. 79 f.

of borrowings from Jewish or Rabbinic law can also be found in the prohibition (in the Qur'ān itself) of lending money for a fixed rate of interest (*ribā*), which Muḥammad presumably took over from the Jews in Madina; the penalty of stoning to death for illicit sexual intercouse (which is not in fact Qur'anic) on the part of anyone who has ever enjoyed a valid marriage; and even the jurisprudential sources (and methods) of *qiyās*, *istiṣlāḥ*, etc.[23] From Byzantine law Muslims adopted the office of the 'inspector of the market', which later developed into that of the *muḥtasib*;[24] from the Sassanian administration they borrowed the concept of the investigation of complaints (*naẓar fi'l-maẓālim*), which gave rise to the Court of Complaints, and the office of 'clerk of the courts' (*kātib*), who became an assistant of the *qāḍī*;[25] and from the Canon law of the Eastern Churchs the principle, still retained in the Ithnā 'Asharī and Ibāḍī law, that adultery constitutes an impediment to marriage.[26] A particularly good example of a distinctively Muslim institution which was originally derived from an alien source, moreover, is provided by the *waqf* system, which was founded on the pious foundations (*piae causae*) of the Eastern Churches but was developed in new ways, and for a variety of different purposes, in Islamic law.[27]

It has often been remarked that, for all their differences in matters of constitutional theory, etc., the detailed law of the Shī'īs and Ibāḍīs does not differ very widely from that of the Sunnīs. For this several reasons may be suggested. To begin with, all Muslims accept the same Qur'ān — although it is true that the Shī'īs complain that a few verses which were particularly favourable to the claims of 'Alī were deliberately omitted, and the followers of the Aghā Khān believe that he can still speak with the divine voice, and thus introduce radical reforms in their law with a freedom denied

[23] *Ibid.*, pp. 13, 15, 21.   [24] *Ibid.*, p. 25.   [25] *Ibid.*, pp. 51 and 21, 25, etc.   [26] *Ibid.*, p. 21.   [27] *Ibid.*, p. 19.

to other Muslims. Neither the Shī'īs nor the Ibāḍīs, moreover, accept the Sunnī books of 'authentic traditions', since the Shī'īs reject any tradition whatever that has not been related by or through one of their Imāms, and the Ibāḍīs also have their own collections; but this, too, does not seem to have caused many major differences in practice. Both the Shī'īs and the Ibāḍīs, again, reject the Sunnī *ijmā'* and *qiyas*, although both communities, for the most part, accept a sort of consensus of their own and make use of a form of legal reasoning which the Shī'īs, for example, call *'aql.* But the fact remains that the different communities were in sufficiently close touch with each other throughout the formative period of Islamic law for the heterodox groups to take over the law which was being developed in the Sunnī schools with only such modifications as their own political or legal theories seemed to demand.[28] Yet it is, I think, fair to accept Professor N. J. Coulson's conclusion that, whereas Sunnī political theory 'represents an amalgam of Islamic principles and pre-Islamic practice – rule by the traditional tribal aristocracy subject to the dictates of the religious law' – Ithnā 'Asharī political theory, on the other hand,

> renounces any connection with pre-Islamic practice and sees the sole source of authority to lie in the Founder-Prophet and his attributes as a religious leader. . . . Juristically as well as politically, Islam meant a re-orientation and modification of existing practice for the Sunnīs, while for the Ithnā 'Asharīs it marked a completely new point of departure.[29]

It is remarkable, however, that in spite of the debt that the Sharī'a – particularly in its Sunnī form – owes to the customary law which preceded it, this law has received virtually no official recognition in Islamic jurisprudence. It is

[28] *Ibid.,* p. 16   [29] *A History of Islamic Law* (Edinburgh University Press, 1964), p. 118.

true that in many parts of the Muslim world local customary
law has not only survived alongside the Shari'a but is
regularly applied in its stead, even by specifically Islamic
courts, in many spheres of life — particularly, perhaps, in the
practice of the markets. But the customary law which forms
the basis of so much of the Islamic law itself is very seldom
acknowledged as such. Instead, it has in most cases been
tacitly incorporated in the Shari'a under one of the recognized sources of Islamic jurisprudence — occasionally by a
verse from the Qur'ān (or the way in which this is interpreted and applied), but much more often under the
authority of some tradition or of *ijmā'* (particularly, of
course, where this is peculiar to some specific area, like the
ijmā' of Madina in Mālikī law).

I have already referred to the way in which Shari'a law
was open, in its earliest stages, to the free current of ideas.
Throughout this period — and, indeed, until about the
middle of the third century of the Hijra — any suitably
qualified jurist had enjoyed the right of independent reasoning: that is, the liberty to use his own judgement as to what
the law ought to be, and to deduce from the original sources
the solution to a new problem. But by the beginning of the
fourth century of the Hijra

> the point had been reached when the scholars of all
> schools felt that all essential questions had been
> thoroughly discussed and finally settled, and a con-
> sensus gradually established itself to the effect that
> from that time onwards no one might be deemed to
> have the necessary qualifications for independent
> reasoning in law, and that all future activity would
> have to be confined to the explanation, application,
> and, at the most, interpretation of the doctrine as it
> had been laid down once and for all. This 'closing of
> the door of *ijtihād*', as it was called, amounted to a

> demand for *taqlīd*, a term which . . . now came to
> mean the unquestioning acceptance of the doctrine of
> established schools and authorities.[30]

It is true that a number of subsequent scholars have claimed
to be *mujtahids* (that is, to have the right to exercise
ijtihād). But this has usually been confined in practice to
comparatively narrow limits, and has never commanded
general assent. Even among the Shī'īs, moreover, who still
accord to some of their scholars the title of *mujtahid*, the
discretion they exercise in practice is far from wide; and in
Sunnī or orthodox Islam the author of even the most
authoritative treatise has, for centuries, been regarded as a
mere *muqallid* (that is, one confined to *taqlīd*). There have,
of course, been developments in the law down the centuries,
many of which can be found in the books of *fatāwā*, or legal
opinions. But the numerous one-time variant opinions in
each of the schools have gradually been eliminated in favour
of a doctrine which is generally accepted, and the law has
become more and more rigid and moribund.

Another factor which has led to rigidity in Islamic law has
been the insistence of al-Ash'arī (who died in the fourth
century of the Hijra) that man is incapable, of himself, of
apprehending the moral quality of human actions without
the enlightenment of divine revelation. No doctrine of
Natural Law would have been acceptable to him: what man
needed was God's direct and explicit revelation. He even
went so far as to deny that such qualities as virtue and vice
exist of themselves, or have any meaning whatever apart
from the divine command or prohibition. God does not
command the good because it is intrinsically good, or forbid
the evil because it is inherently evil. On the contrary, it is
exclusively the divine command or prohibition which makes
actions virtuous or vicious; indeed, had the divine revelation

---

[30] Schacht, *Introduction*, pp. 70 f.

been different, then virtue would have become vice, and vice virtue. But, as we have seen among the Schoolmen,[31] there has always been a variety of opinions on this matter within the fold of Islam. The Mu'tazilis,[32] for instance, took a very different view, for they have always asserted that human acts are either good or bad in themselves, and that God commanded the good because it was good and forbade the evil because it was evil. More, they held that in some cases human reason can perceive, independently of divine revelation, that an act is virtuous or vicious *per se*. In such cases God's revelation merely confirms what man could have apprehended of himself, whereas in other matters he is completely dependent on divine enlightenment. And yet others, such as the Mâtaridis and many Ḥanafî jurists, took up an intermediate position. They agreed with the Mu'tazilis that human acts are intrinsically good or evil, and that human reason can in some cases discern this. Unlike the Mu'tazilis, however, they refused – in general – to admit that man had any obligation to do what was right or abstain from what was wrong until this was made plain by the divine command or prohibition. But it was the more extreme view of al-Ash'ari which predominated in orthodox Islam.

It follows, of course, that the Sharî'a covers the whole of life, and that there is little difference between law and morality in Islam. It is true that one can at times discern, behind the moral categories of good or evil, a more specifically legal category of valid or invalid. It is morally wrong, for instance, for a man to divorce his wife without adequate reason; but if he pronounces the repudiation in the proper form this constitutes a valid divorce, however sinful it may be. It is also true that a large part of the Sharî'a could never be enforced by any human court, but must always depend for sanction on the bar of eternity. Many Muslims, for example, classify all human actions in one of five different

[31] Cf. pp. 36 f. above.   [32] Cf. pp 94, 159 below.

categories: what is explicitly commanded; what is rec-
ommended but not expressly enjoined; what is left legally indifferent; what is reprobated but not explicitly prohibited;
and what is expressly forbidden. Clearly, then, it is only the
first and last of these categories which could ever be enforced by human courts; and it is only the middle
category — what the divine law has left 'legally indifferent' —
that represents the proper sphere of human regulations.

Very few Muslim governments have tried to enforce the
Sharī'a strictly in the life of the markets, and virtually none
of them have been content to leave the maintenance of law
and order exclusively to the *qāḍīs'* courts — committed as
these are, in theory at least, to the enforcement of the
criminal provisions of the Sharī'a exclusively by those
principles of procedure and proof which the Sharī'a itself
prescribes. As a result, both the *qāḍīs* and the legal scholars have
commonly conceded that there is a sphere in which the ruler
may properly exercise a lawful discretion. This is called
siyāsa shar'iyya, and provides the primary foundation for
the widespread legislation which has transformed the
Muslim world in recent years. This has commonly been
characterized by two main features: first, by the withdrawal
of commercial and criminal law — and, in fact, almost
everything outside what might be termed 'family law' in the
widest connotation of that term — from the scope of the
specifically Islamic courts, and its consignment instead to
new 'secular' courts to administer under a series of statutory
enactments which are largely (although often not exclusively) of alien origin; and, secondly, by the introduction of
some radical changes even in the sphere of family law itself
by one or more of four expedients which, it is claimed, do
not deprive it of its basically Islamic character. One of these
is a procedural device which makes no pretension to affect
any substantive change in the Islamic law as such, but
which radically excludes its application by the courts in

specified circumstances. Another (which constitutes far the most widely used expedient of all) represents an eclectic device by means of which the executive or legislature prescribes which opinion of some recognized school or scholar of the past shall be followed in given circumstances; and this principle is often stretched to include opinions drawn from 'heterodox' schools or highly individualistic jurists, or even to cover the resort to *talfīq* (patching), by means of which part of one reputable opinion of the past is so combined with part of another as to produce a result which neither of the authorities concerned would have approved, however respectable the lineage of its component parts may be. A third expedient – to which recourse is normally had only when no authority of the past can be quoted in support – is a new interpretation of some basic text in either the Qur'ān or *sunna*. And the fourth such expedient represents a law or administrative order which is usually based on one of the three devices already mentioned, but which occasionally contents itself with the statement that it is 'not contrary to Islamic law'.

The opponents of these reforms have always been quick to claim that they are contrary to the principle of *ijmā'*; that they represent a hotch-potch of provisions which frequently rest on mutually contradictory principles; and that they constitute a thinly veiled cover for what is really a new exercise of the right of *ijtihād* – and an *ijtihād* which rests on singularly inconsistent and unscholarly foundations.[33] More fundamentally still, they assert that the basic nature of the Sharī'a has been changed; for whereas, in the past, the Sharī'a represented a God-given blueprint to which both Caliph and slave, sultan and subject were, alike, bound to attempt to conform, it is now the State which legislates as it pleases, and which even presumes to decree which parts of the Sharī'a are to be applied by the courts, and how this is to

[33] See pp. 87 f. above.

be done. This last charge, moreover, is virtually un-answerable – except by a frank admission that times have changed, that parts of the Shari'a are no longer suitable for modern life, and that in those parts where a variety of inter-pretations are possible it is essential for the State to specify which one is to be applied. Even so, the fact remains that, while the Shari'a had never, in practice, exercised the monopoly of authority and obedience often ascribed to it in theory, it had certainly provided a canon – to which lip ser-vice, at least, was paid by all – against which every man's actions could be measured. In this respect, at least, it had fulfilled a role somewhat similar to that of 'Natural Law'.

Whereas, moreover, a failure to observe its provisions was in general regarded as human and venial, any questioning of its authority represented rank apostasy and unbelief. Joseph Schacht did not exaggerate when he insisted that 'Islamic law is the epitome of Islamic thought, the most typical manifestation of the Islamic way of life, the core and kernel of Islam itself',[34] nor was Sir Hamilton Gibb indulg-ing in hyperbole when he affirmed that it had always rep-resented the master science in the Muslim world and the most effective agent in holding the social fabric of Islam compact and secure through all the fluctuations of political fortune.[35] It is only natural, of course, that independent States should differ among themselves in the degree to which they have felt this law had to be brought into conformity with the facts of modern life – particularly when some of those States are regarded as 'reactionary' and others as 'revolutionary'; but the fact remains that the cement which once bound them together has now become very loose and uneven.

In the old days, however, Muslim education used always to rest on two sciences, not one: on both theology and the

[34] *Introduction*, p. 1.   [35] *Mohammedanism* (OUP, 2nd ed., London, 1953), pp. 9-11.

sacred law. It is fair enough to describe the law as the 'master science', since Islam has always been much more positive, detailed and authoritative about the way of life that the Creator has prescribed for his creatures than about the nature and characteristics of the Creator himself. It is, perhaps, symptomatic in this context that there has always been more concurrence and emphasis in Islam about the five (or six)[36] 'Pillars of Religion' — all of which constitute ways in which men should behave — than about the six 'Articles of Belief'[37]; and it is certainly significant that Muslim religious leaders, like Jewish Rabbis, have been primarily lawyers,[38] while it is only among the Ṣūfīs that we find anything approaching an 'ordained' ministry. All the same, disputes about matters of theology were far from rare. In the fragmentation of Islam between Sunnīs, Shī'īs and Khawārij, for example, political, theological and subsequently legal issues all played their part; and here, as in subsequent disputes, one of the major questions was 'who is a Muslim?' To this the fanatical Shī'ī was wont to reply 'Only he who recognizes the true Imām', while the Khārijī insisted that it was only he whose 'works' went hand in hand with his faith — and this, too, had a political as well as a theological aspect, for it was bound up with people's attitude to the Umayyad dynasty. But if the Khawārij were far too extreme

[36] The five 'Pillars of Religion' on which there is general agreement are the recitation of the Creed as a Confession of Faith, the performance of the ritual Prayers, the giving of Alms, the observance of the Ramaḍān Fast, and (where feasible) the Pilgrimage to Mecca. But some Muslims (e.g. the Khawārij) included the Holy War (or *jihād*) as a sixth Pillar.
[37] Belief in God, his Angels, his Prophets, his inspired Books, his Decrees and the Last Day.   [38] Cf. pp. 98, 104 below and pp. 57 f. above. *One* reason why both Judaism and Islam have had much more to say about what God commands men to do than what he himself is like was the result of the Aristotelian philosophy which prevailed during the Scholastic period. This affected Christian thought, too; and it was primarily the Incarnation which saved Christian doctrine from the narrow confines of the *via negativa*.

in insisting that any unrepented sin constituted apostasy, was it right to go to the other extreme and hold that faith alone was sufficient for salvation, irrespective of a man's behaviour or his political stance? One answer to this question was provided by the Murji'ites – that is, those who deferred or postponed any such judgement until it was pronounced by God himself on the Day of Judgement. But another early Muslim sect was more exclusively theological in origin – for it turned on the age-old controversy about predestination and free-will. The more puritan wing pointed to a string of Qur'anic verses

> which proclaim human responsibility and declare that men will be recompensed at the Judgement according to their works and their deserts; man is therefore free to choose for himself, and does so by the power which God has created in him. This was the doctrine of the Qadarites, the 'Abilitarians', as against the absolute Predestinarians.[39]

At the beginning of the second century of the Hijra a group of Qadarites 'separated themselves' in order to take up a neutral position in regard to whether a Muslim who committed a flagrant sin was a believer or an unbeliever. Such was the origin of the Mu'tazila,[40] to whom passing reference has already been made; and it was among them that the beginnings arose of an apologetic and scholastic theology, called in Arabic *kalām* or 'discussion'. This seems to have been primarily aimed at two main purposes: at 'asserting the unity and creatorship of God against non-Muslim opponents, dualists of various kinds, sceptics, and the Hellenistic philosophy which maintained the eternity of the world'; and at maintaining the Qadarite doctrine of human freedom against its Muslim opponents.[41] Their doctrines

---

[39] Hamilton Gibb, in *The Concise Encyclopedia of Living Faiths*, pp. 183f.   [40] p. 89 above.   [41] Cf. Gibb, *op. cit.*, p. 184.

found favour with the Caliph al-Ma'mūn, among others, and he established a 'House of Wisdom' in Baghdad in order to organize the production of translations of Greek philosophic works into Arabic. But it was in their insistence that God must, by his very nature, always do what is intrinsically right and most beneficial for his creatures; that God's attributes must be regarded as *identical* with his divine Essence, 'purified from every shade of createdness or occasionalism',[42] and thus interpreted in a largely negative sense; and that the Qur'ān could not, therefore, be regarded as either 'eternal' or 'uncreated' — that they came into sharp conflict with the 'orthodox'. But it took nearly a century

before the orthodox realized that reasoned arguments must be met not by slogans but by reasoned arguments on the other side. Early in the fourth century AH (about AD 920) there emerged the beginnings of an 'orthodox *Kalām*', associated with the names of al-Ash'arī[43] of Baghdad and al-Mātarīdī of Samarqand. Methodologically it took over, as was inevitable, many of the bases of the Mu'tazilite *Kalām*, but it rejected the Mu'tazilite claim to establish human reason as the ultimate criterion of religious truth. True, the blessed will not see God in Paradise as a spatially-defined Being, but they will see him nevertheless, in some manner which human reason and experience cannot specify. True, the Qur'ān, as a written book and as recited by human agency, is created, but its quality as the Speech of God is the same as that of his other attributes, existing in his Essence and therefore uncreated. True, there are in the Qur'ān a number of anthropomorphic metaphors, but they express actions or attributes of which we, as human beings, can know neither the nature nor the manner, and they are not to

[42] *Ibid.*   [43] Cp. p. 88 above.

be wished away by simple or laborious philological exercises or conceits.[44]

Even this, however, went much further than many of the Muslim populace were prepared to go. Instead, they were content to accept these mysteries 'without asking "How?"' and to affirm that the eternal attributes of God in relation to his divine Essence were '*lā dahātahu wa lā ghayrahu*' (that is, not identical with it, nor separable from it).

But there were three other groups with which the orthodox felt compelled to contend: the *falāsifa*, or disciples of Hellenistic philosophy, represented especially by Avicenna and Averroes (or Ibn Sīnā and Ibn Rushd); the extreme Ismāʿīlīs, whose doctrine of emanations, when developed along Gnostic lines, enabled them to confer a divine authority on their Imāms by linking them with the Active Intellect of the philosophers; and the Ṣūfīs, or mystics, who aspired to a direct knowledge of God (*kashf*), or even identification with him (*ittiḥād*). The answer to all three was largely provided by the towering figure of al-Ghazzālī[45] — but in very different ways. He probed the arguments of the philosophers and ruthlessly refuted both their methods and their conclusions in a scathing work entitled *Tahāfut al-Falāsifa* ('The Collapse of the Philosophers'), for he found their reasoning barren and their deductions both mistaken and misleading.[46] He also carefully examined the doctrine of the Taʿlimīs, a group of extreme Ismāʿīlīs, and found their teaching eminently unsatisfactory. Try as he would, he could not understand their alleged mysteries. They would repeat *ad nauseam* formulae they had learnt by rote, but they seemed to know little or nothing else. So his trained mind lost patience with their shallow reasonings and fanci-

---

[44] Gibb, *op. cit.*, p. 185.　　　[45] Died in AD 1111.　　　[46] Cf. D. B. Macdonald, *Muslim Theology, Jurisprudence and Constitutional Theory* (Charles Scribner's Sons, New York, 1903), pp. 219-224 and 229 f.; Gibb, *op. cit.*, pp. 187 ff.

ful assertions, and he wrote several books against them. With the Ṣūfis, on the other hand, he took an entirely different course. He had himself plumbed the depths of intellectual scepticism, so he started to study the books and teachings of the mystics again (for he had been superficially acquainted with them from his youth) with real avidity; and it soon became clear to him that he must be initiated as a mystic himself — live their life and share their ecstatic exercises — if he was to reach his goal. It was not long, moreover, before he became convinced that it was the Ṣūfis who were on the true and only path to an experimental knowledge of God, and accepted the validity of their ecstatic revelations. But he realized that it was both erroneous and dangerous to describe their nearness to God in terms of *ḥulūl* (fusion of being), *ittiḥād* (identification) or *wuṣūl* (union).[47]

The fact is that, while the earliest Muslim mysticism had taken the form of asceticism, largely inspired by the dread of Hell, it was soon exposed to many extraneous influences — Christian, Gnostic, Neo-Platonic and Eastern (whether in the form of Buddhism[49] or certain Hindu concepts). With many of its devotees, therefore, an earnest quest for *communion* with God had become transformed into an extravagant doctrine of essential *union* or even *identity* with him (almost after the manner of the Advaita Vedānta). This was accentuated by the practice of using a variety of means to heighten the psychological effect of the continuous invocation (*dhikr*) of the name of God to induce auto-hypnosis or a state of trance, in the course of which they would at times make statements which were exceedingly offensive to orthodox Muslims. It was thus that in AD 922 an example was made of one of the most notorious theosophists,

[47] Cf. Macdonald, *op. cit.*, pp. 224-228.   [48] Especially, perhaps, in conjunction with the teaching of the pseudo Dionysius the Areopagite. [49] Cf. the partial resemblance between the Ṣūfī concept of *al-fanā'* and that of *Nirvāṇa*.

al-Ḥusayn bin Manṣūr al-Ḥallāj, by putting him to a cruel
death for asserting 'I am the Truth'. But there were other
Ṣūfīs on whom no shadow of unorthodoxy seems ever to have
rested. Such, for example, was al-Junayd, who insisted that
no man could be a true Ṣūfī unless he held firmly to the
Qur'ān and the *sunna* of the Prophet.[50] So it was, perhaps,
al-Ghazzālī's major achievement to bring Ṣūfism within the
somewhat arid confines of orthodox Islam, and to open up
orthodox thought to the acceptance of the Ṣūfism which was
truly Islamic.

But it is time to sum up. If, as we have seen, Judaism can
be accounted a religion in which the paramount emphasis
falls on the Law of God rather than the Love of God, then
this is still more true of Islam. In the Old Testament, as we
have seen, the law is set in the context of God's covenant
with his people and represents the response which God ex-
pects from them to an initiative which he has already taken
in sheer grace. Tender passages recur, moreover, in which
God is portrayed as a father who teaches his child to walk, a
shepherd who carries his lamb in his arms, a lover who woos
his beloved, and even a husband who longs for his unfaithful
wife to return to him. In Islam, by contrast, the constant
reference is to God as sovereign Lord (*Rabb*), and man as
his servant or slave (*'abd*). It is significant in this context, I
think, that 'Love', or 'Loving', finds no place among the
seven 'Eternal Attributes' of God (*al-Ṣifāt al-Azaliyya*) to
which Muslim theology so often refers.

But this is certainly not to suggest that the concept of the
love of God is wholly lacking in Islam. A number of phrases
from the Qur'ān itself could be quoted to refute any such
assertion. In Sūra 2:191, for example, we read that 'Allah
loveth those who do well'; in 2:222 that 'Allah loveth those
who turn continually in penitence, and loveth those who
keep themselves pure'; in 3:70 that 'Allah loveth those

[50] Cf. Gibb, *op. cit.*, p. 190.

who act piously'; and in 5:46 that 'Allah loveth those who
act with fairness'; etc. These verses, it is true, affirm the love
of God only for those who in some measure deserve it, and
there are far more which assert that God does *not* love those
who do not; but against this must be balanced verses like
5:43, which states that 'if anyone repent after his wrongdoing and set things right, Allah will repent towards him;
Allah is forgiving, compassionate'. In all these verses the
Arabic word for 'love' is the verb *yaḥibb*; but a noun for
'love' and an adjective for 'loving' from another root (*wudd*
and *wadūd*) are used in 19:96 which states: 'verily for those
who have believed and done works of righteousness will the
Merciful appoint love', and in both 11:92 and 85:14, which
affirm, respectively: 'Verily my Lord is compassionate, loving' and 'He is the Forgiving, the Loving'.[51]

Muslim piety, moreover, largely centres round the constant repetition of the ninety-nine 'Beautiful Names' of God.
Far the best known of these are the first two, 'The Compassionate, the Merciful' (*al-Raḥmān al-Raḥīm*), which are
coupled together at the head of every Sūra except one in the
Qur'ān. The two words in Arabic both come from the same
root, and when they are conjoined in this way Dr Kenneth
Cragg writes that

> the first should probably be regarded rather as a noun
> than an adjective, with the second qualifying it: 'The
> Merciful Mercier' or 'the Compassionate Compas-
> sionator'. The sequence is not mere repetition. The
> *Raḥmān* is the One Who is in His character merciful.
> The *Raḥīm* is He in merciful action. He Who is merci-
> ful behaves mercifully. His mercy is of His essence, and
> also of His deed.[52]

This sounds as though it should convince any Muslim of

---

[51] The translation of all these verses has been taken from *The Qur'ān*, by
Richard Bell (T. and T. Clark, Edinburgh, 1937).   [52] *The Call of the
Minaret* (OUP, New York, 1956), p. 40.

the unchanging love of God, and prompts the question why this concept is so muted in Islam. Part of the reason may, perhaps, be found in the fact that the last of the above quoted references goes on to describe God as 'The Occupant of the Throne, the Glorious, the Doer of what he intendeth' — which, in Kenneth Cragg's words, represents 'the perpetual condition of all the attributes. They are to be understood finally as characteristics of the Divine will rather than laws of his nature.[53] Put more starkly, the salient impression one gets from Islamic theology as a whole is that of the sovereign Lord for whose mercy one may certainly hope, but of which one can never be assured. And on this, as on so many subjects, the Traditions record a wide variety of statements which Muḥammad is alleged to have made. In one, for example, he is recorded as stating that the Almighty has said 'My servant does not draw near to Me with anything more loved by Me than the religious duties I have imposed upon him, and My servant continues to draw near to Me with supererogatory works so that I shall love him. . . . Were he to ask [something] of Me, I would surely give it to him; and were he to ask Me for refuge, I would surely grant him it'.[54] Yet, in another, we are told that 'when God resolved to create the human race, He took into His hands a mass of earth, the same whence all mankind were to be formed, and in which they after a manner pre-existed; and having then divided the clod into two equal portions, He threw the one half into hell, saying, "These to eternal fire, and I care not"; and projected the other half into heaven, adding, "and these to Paradise, and I care not".'[55] I am not, of course suggesting for a moment that either of these traditions are

---

[53] *Ibid.*   [54] An-Nawawī's *Forty Hadith*, translated by Ezzedin Ibrahim and Denys Johnson-Davies (2nd ed., The Holy Koran Publishing House, Damascus, 1977), p. 118 (from al-Bukhārī's *al-Ṣaḥīḥ*).   [55] Hughes' *Dictionary of Islam* (London, W. H. Allen & Co., 1895), p. 148 (from *Mishkātu'l-Maṣābīḥ, Bābu'l-Qadr*).

authentic, but they serve to illustrate two deeply rooted Muslim beliefs: the first, that the faithful worshipper may, indeed, *hope* for God's mercy; and the second that, in the last resort, all depends on the divine decree, and that God is too transcendent to be affected in any way by man's behaviour or destiny. To think of him as being made sad by man's indifference, sin and ultimate damnation, or glad by man's response, obedience and salvation, would derogate from his utter transcendence and self-sufficiency (*tanzīh*). It seems probable, moreover, that this was a concept of God which was absorbed by Islam — as, also, in part at least, by Judaism and Christianity in the Scholastic era — from Aristotelian philosophy, for it is far removed from the language of the Bible. But it certainly looks somewhat less alien in Muslim theology (in which teaching about the love of God was largely ignored, and even al-Juwaynī, Imām al-Ḥaramayn, is reported to have said that, strictly speaking, God can neither love nor be loved)[56] than it does in the religion of the Cross.

There is, moreover, another basic doctrine of Islam — itself closely connected with the concept of transcendence — which deprives the Qur'anic testimony to the love and mercy of God of much of its natural import. I refer to the doctrine of *al-mukhālafa*, or the utter difference between God and man. This means, to quote Dr Kenneth Cragg once more, that

> Terms taken from human meanings — and there are of course no others — were said to be used of God with a difference. They did not convey the human connotation but were used in those senses feasible of God. When the further question was pressed: What then do they convey as applied to God? no precise answer was capable of being formulated. Islam here falls back

[56] A. S. Tritton, *Muslim Theology* (Luzac, London, 1947), pp. 9 and 185.

upon a final agnosticism. Terms must be used if there
is to be religion at all. But only God knows what they
signify. Muslim theology coined the related phrases
Bilā Kaif and *Bilā Tashbih*. We use these names 'without knowing how' they apply and without implying any
human similarity.[57]

But if we may not conclude that divine compassion and
mercy are in some degree analagous, although far superior,
to human compassion and mercy, then the 'Beautiful
Names' of God — including, of course, *al-Raḥmān
al-Raḥīm* — may, indeed, be beautiful sounds in a Muslim's
ear, but remain devoid of any intelligible content.

It is no matter for surprise, therefore, that the more ardent spirits in the Muslim community have so often turned
to the Ṣūfīs, or mystics of Islam, for a spiritual satisfaction
that reaches to the heart. The daily ritual of Islam and the
stern demands of the law provide little to quicken the pulse
or fire the emotions, and the Muslim is normally left to find
what spiritual sustenance he can in the somewhat arid
pastures of *naql*, or the teachings of tradition, and *'aql*, or
the deductions of reason. Neither provides any real access to
the person or nature of God, except in the form of
philosophical abstractions; so many Muslims have turned,
all down the ages, to *kashf*, or the direct revelation and
knowledge of God which the mystics have always sought and
commended.

Islamic mysticism, as we have seen, seems to have been
present in some measure from the very first. Initially it was
largely native to Islam, and took the form of extreme
ascetiscism — inspired, to a considerable degree, by a profound fear of God. The name Ṣūfī can probably be traced to
the Arabic word for wool (*ṣūf*) in reference to the coarse
woollen garments which these wandering monks and hermits habitually wore. They renounced the world; they often

[57] *Op. cit.*, pp. 55.

relied wholly on God, or the generosity of other Muslims, for their sustenance (*tawakkul*); and they sought the direct illumination of God by the sustained remembrance and repetition of his name. For this they could find a good Qur'anic basis, for in Sūra 33:41 believers are exhorted to 'remember (*dhikr*) God often'. But one of the chief criticisms of the Ṣūfīs, from the first, was that they neglected the five canonical prayers in favour of their own practice of individual and community prayer of a much less formal nature. Comparatively soon, moreover, the somewhat negative renunciation and penitence of the ascetic began to blossom into the rapture of what the ecstatic believed to be a direct experience of God — so much so that, for many Ṣūfīs, the term *tawḥīd* (which primarily represents the basic affirmation that God is One)[58] came to be used of the 'Ṣūfī experience of *fanā*', or ecstatic annihilation, in which the self is lost in the one'.[58] This is not the place to discuss the very disparate sources from which Muslim mysticism eventually derived its doctrines and to which passing reference has already been made;[59] but it is clear that the basically Islamic mysticism to which I have already referred was, almost from the first, enriched by contact with Christian hermits and ascetics, and that it was not long before the emanations of Plotinus, the ideals of Plato and the spheres of Aristotle began to be coupled with the seven-storied heaven of Muhammad.[60] Another powerful source came from the East, chiefly through centres of Buddhist activity in Iraq and Iràn. As a result some Ṣūfīs became deeply imbued with pantheism and monism; but others cultivated an ardent love for a personal God, whom they not infrequently called their Beloved (*ḥabīb*).

---

[58] Cf. A. K. Cragg, *The Christian and Other Religions* (Mowbray, London, 1977), p. 46.   [59] Cf. p. 97 above.   [60] Cf. D. B. Macdonald, *Muslim Theology, Jurisprudence and Constitutional Theory* (Charles Scribner, New York, 1903), p. 164.

This is the aspect of Ṣūfism which concerns us in this context, for there can be no doubt that many of the mystics of Islam gave a primary place to love and – as their opponents continually pointed out – sat very lightly by law. It seems clear, however, that the major emphasis was always on man's love for God as his highest good, rather than on the undeserved love of God for his wayward creatures. It would certainly be wrong, however, to suggest that the lover's passionate desire for his Beloved, and his ecstatic sense of union with him, do not involve some concept of a responsive love from the divine object of his affection. It is not for nothing that Ṣūfīs concentrate on the Qur'anic phrase: 'a people whom He loveth and who love Him' (65:59).

Some will no doubt remark that my references to, and discussion of, the Islamic preoccupation with the Law of God rather than with any understanding of his Love have taken up what may well appear an undue proportion of time and space in this chapter. To that I can only reply that I believe that this represents a substantially accurate reflection of the place that the divine law and the divine love occupy, respectively, in Islamic thought and writing. Nor is this an isolated phenomenon or matter of chance. On the contrary, Professor J. W. Sweetman has justly observed that

> Muslims have trod the *via negativa* to the bitter end,
> and even their acceptance of a doctrine of revelation is
> limited by the acceptance that here is only a revelation
> *from* God and not a revelation primarily *of Himself*.[61]

Islam is, indeed, exceedingly rich in what Muslims believe to be divine disclosures of God's will for man, but the mystery of God himself – his person, nature and character – remain shrouded in largely negative abstractions.

[61] J. W. Sweetman, *Islam and Christian Theology* (Part Two, Vol. 2, Lutterworth Press, London, 1967), p. 327. Yet Sweetman does quote the exclamation of the great Muslim poet, Jalālu'd-Dīn Rūmī: 'Had it not been for Love's sake how should I have bestowed existence on the Heavens? (*Ibid.*)

CHAPTER 4

The Law of God and
the Love of God in Christianity

When we turn to the New Testament, we are at once struck by an apparent ambivalence in the attitude to the Law taken both by Paul and even by Jesus himself. It is obvious, for instance, that Jesus made a sharp distinction (largely alien, as we have seen, to his Jewish contemporaries) between the written law, as the commandment of God, and the oral law, as the 'tradition of the elders'. An incident is recorded in both Mark 7 and Matthew 15, for example, in which Jesus was criticized by the Pharisees and teachers of the law because his disciples came in from the market and proceeded to eat without first ceremonially washing their hands. But he was wholly unmoved, and at once went over to the offensive by telling them that they, on their part, had completely nullified and set aside the commandment of God, in the Decalogue itself, that a man should 'honour' his father and mother, by the expedient of decreeing that, should he say that his goods were vowed or dedicated to the Temple ('Corban'), he was forthwith legally forbidden to use them for the relief of his parents' needs. Then, for good measure, he took the opportunity to explain to his disciples that a man is made spiritually unclean not by the omission of some outward or ceremonial requirement, but by the evil thoughts and deeds which well up from his inner being or

105

subconscious mind. 'Nothing outside a man', he said, 'can make him "unclean".' Years later, moreover, the redactor of this Gospel had the insight to remark that 'In saying this, Jesus declared all foods "clean".'[1]

As can be seen in this incident and the comments to which it gave rise, it was not only evasions and perversions of the written law which Jesus condemned, but also those hair-splitting refinements and legalistic additions which changed a Jew's attempt to keep the law of his God from a joy and delight into an almost impossible burden. Another example of this may be found in Luke 6:1, where the Pharisees criticized the fact that, when Jesus was walking through the grainfields with his disciples on a Sabbath day, 'his disciples began to pick some heads of corn, rub them in their hands, and eat the kernels'. This was not regarded as stealing, since Leviticus 23:25 clearly states that: 'If you enter your neighbour's grainfield, you *may* pick the kernels with your hands, but you must not put a sickle to his standing grain'; so the only offence committed by the disciples was against the Rabbinic decision that to pluck and eat a few ears of corn was equivalent to breaking the divine command not to engage in the work of harvesting and threshing on the Sabbath. It was this sort of attitude which prompted Jesus to make the categorical claim that 'The Son of Man is Lord of the Sabbath'[2] – or, more generally, to state the principle that 'The Sabbath was made for man, and not man for the Sabbath'.[3] In a still wider reference, it was this rigorous insistence on minutiae which moved him to give his gracious invitation: 'Come to me, all you who are weary and burdened, and I will give you rest. Take my yoke upon you and learn from me, for I am gentle and humble in heart, and you will find rest for your souls. For my yoke is easy

[1] Mark 7:1-20. Here at verse 19. Cf. Matt. 15:1-19.   [2] Luke 6:5.
[3] Mark 2:27.

and my burden is light'.[4]

Now there can be no doubt whatever that Jesus was referring, in this passage, to the 'yoke' and 'burden' of the Law –
as, indeed, when he rebuked the lawyers by saying that they
'tie up heavy loads and put them on men's shoulders, but
they themselves are not willing to lift a finger to move
them'.[5] It was not that he was suggesting for a moment that
his teaching was less morally exacting than the Mosaic Law.
On the contrary, it set a far higher standard, as he often
made plain. What he meant was that his teaching was essentially different from the innumerable, pettifogging details of
the Rabbinic law, and that the 'New Covenant' which he
had come to inaugurate would change the whole question of
law-keeping from a vain attempt to observe an external
Code, which demanded an unwilling (and even impossible)
obedience, into a glad response, enabled by his Spirit, to the
inward promptings of love. That was why he could say that
'my yoke is easy and my burden is light'; and why John, years
later, could confirm that 'his commandments are not
burdensome'.[6]

It seems probable, moreover, that the fact that Matthew
has collected together in chapters 5-7 moral principles
which were almost certainly enunciated on a number of different occasions,[7] that the setting was on a 'mountain', and
that Jesus is depicted as 'sitting'[8] in the way normally
adopted by the Rabbis when teaching, indicates that this
discourse was designed by Matthew to represent Jesus, as
the second Moses, promulgating the Law – or, rather, the
principles – of his Kingdom. That he did not in any way in-
tend to abrogate the Mosaic Law is made perfectly clear by
his categorical statement: 'Do not think that I have come to
abolish the Law or the Prophets; I have not come to abolish

---

[4] Matt. 11:28-30. Cf. Mishnah, Aboth 3:5: 'He that taketh on himself the
yoke of the Law.' Cf. also Babylonian Talmud, Sanhedrin, 94b.
[5] Luke 11:46.   [6] I John 5:3.   [7] Luke 6:20 ff.   [8] Matt. 5:1.

them but to fulfil them. I tell you the truth, until heaven
and earth disappear, not the smallest letter, not the least
stroke of a pen, will by any means disappear from the Law
until everything is accomplished.' It can, indeed, be
cogently maintained that his teaching in this discourse does
not contradict the Mosaic law as such. Instead, it may be
seen as bringing out its deeper meaning and showing his
disapproval of the narrow and legalistic interpretation
which had so often been put upon it. But while, as Professor
Tasker insists,[9] he clearly regarded the Old Testament as
possessing permanent validity as the Word of God, it is also
clear that he regarded his own teaching as having decisive
authority.

This is why, when dealing with Judaism in Chapter 2, I
was at pains to point out that the distinction made in the
seventh of the 'Thirty Nine Articles' between the 'moral',
the 'ceremonial' and the 'civil' law is still of great spiritual
value, however little ancient Israel would have understood this classification; for Jesus may clearly be said
to have 'fulfilled' these three parts of the Mosaic Law in
totally different ways. He fulfilled the moral law primarily
by his life of perfect obedience to its dictates and by his
death of vicarious atonement on behalf of those who had
failed to keep it; but he also fulfilled it by giving it a wider
scope of moral application, and by re-imposing its requirements — not as a means of salvation, which was never
its purpose, but as a divinely revealed way of life — upon his
disciples. Again, he fulfilled the ceremonial law by being
himself the substance and anti-type to which the shadows
and types of the sacrificial system all pointed forward. So,
once he had died and been raised again, there was no longer
any place for the ceremonial law except as an abiding
witness to the meaning of what he had done. As for the civil
and criminal law, both of which were intended for the

[9] R. V. G. Tasker, *St Matthew* (Tyndale Press, London, 1961), pp. 64 f.

human government of a nomadic tribe which was soon to be transformed into a pastoral community, this too had been 'fulfilled' when the 'Kingdom of God' had been taken from them 'and given to a people who will produce its fruit'.[10] This 'people' no longer represent an ethnic nation but the whole company of the redeemed – which will one day be gathered in from 'every nation, tribe, people and language',[11] and which, in the meantime, is naturally subject to the civil and criminal laws of the nation-states to which its members belong. I suppose, moreover, that it is possible to regard the dietary regulations of ancient Israel as either 'ceremonial' or 'civil'; but in either case they have now fulfilled their purpose and are no longer applicable – in somewhat the same way, perhaps, as that in which the Jewish Sabbath has been changed into the Christian Sunday as the day we now set aside for rest and worship, but without the detailed regulations of Old Testament or Rabbinic law.

I have already remarked that these distinctions between different parts of the law would have been largely meaningless to Israel of old. Instead, the Jews regarded the law as a whole as a corpus of 'instruction' (*Torah*), given them by God for their good, which they must do their best to obey out of loving gratitude for his grace in establishing his covenant with them. But in course of time, as P. S. Watson insists,

> its observance came to be thought of less as their grateful response to him and the keeping of their part of the covenant, than as the means of securing his gracious regard for them and ensuring their claim to a part in the covenant. In post-exilic Judaism, conformity with the requirements of the law became the way of salvation. By strict observance of the law, men would be holy and righteous as God is holy and righteous, in

[10] Matthew 21:43.   [11] Revelation 7:9.

order to pass the test of his judgement and merit a place in his everlasting kingdom. The law became in fact the mediator between man and God.[12]

This is spelt out in detail, and with unmistakable clarity, in the teaching of Paul, who could see it in the full light of Good Friday, Easter and Pentecost. So his agonizing indictment of Israel[13] was that, instead of submitting to the way of justification or righteousness which God had himself planned for them, they were earnestly pursuing a way of self-vindication by the meticulous observance of all the vast proliferation of precepts and prohibitions in both the written and oral law. The tragic result was their utter failure to recognize the one mediator between God and man, who was also the 'end of the law' in the double sense of being the one to whom it led and in whom all its purposes were fulfilled.

But an alternative view of post-exilic Judaism, strongly advocated by E. P. Sanders,[14] G. F. Moore[15] and others, is that the Jews of the New Testament period were intent on their meticulous keeping of the law not as a means of earning salvation, but as a demonstration that they (and they alone) were indeed God's chosen people, living under a covenant of pure grace. This view would fit in excellently with the argument between Jesus and 'the Jews', recorded in John 8:33, in which they insisted that they were the true 'seed' or descendents of Abraham; and also with Paul's indictment, in Romans 2:17, of Jews who 'rely on the law and brag about (their) relationship to God'. It would, moreover, only marginally affect Paul's heartbroken indictment in Romans 10:1-4 and my comments on this in the previous paragraph. The sole difference would be that, on the one view, they were being kept back from Christ by their

---

[12] *A Dictionary of Christian Theology* (ed. Alan Richardson, SCM Press, London, 1969), p. 190.   [13] Romans 10:1-4.   [14] *Paul and Palestinian Judaism* (SCM, London, 1977).   [15] *Judaism* (Harvard University Press, Cambridge, 1927).

determination to vindicate themselves through the law, and, on the other, by their presumptuous reliance on their coven-ant status as Jews.

But much of this was already implicit in the teaching of Jesus, although the time of full revelation had then not yet come. In the Sermon on the Mount, for example, he taught that the commandments in the Decalogue which forbade murder and adultery were far more extensive in their im-plications than Israel had ever realized; that the injunction in the Pentateuch to 'love your neighbour', when shorn of the very questionable gloss 'and hate your enemy', set a standard of love for friend and foe alike which was wholly impossible of attainment by fallen man; and that any hope of entrance into God's heavenly kingdom on the basis of their own righteousness would entail a quality of life in-finitely more exacting than that of the Pharisees and teachers of the law.[16] This is, of course, very similar to the answer he gave to the 'expert in the law' who asked him what he must do to inherit eternal life. 'What is written in the Law?', Jesus replied, 'How do you read it?' 'Love the Lord your God with all your heart and with all your soul and with all your strength and with all your mind' and 'Love your neighbour as yourself', he said. 'You have answered cor-rectly', Jesus replied. 'Do this and you will live'.[17] No wonder his questioner began to prevaricate!

But in the teaching of Paul we find an attitude of am-bivalence towards the Law which was not only apparent but stark. As 'a Hebrew of the Hebrews; in regard to the law, a Pharisee,'[18] he naturally had no doubt that 'the law is holy, and the commandment is holy, righteous and good'.[19] He could even assert that 'in my inner being, I delight in God's law'.[20] But the trouble was that he simply could not obey it. The commandment 'Do not covet' had opened his

[16] Matthew 5:20. [17] Luke 10:25 ff. [18] Philippians 3:5.
[19] Romans 7:12. [20] Romans 7:22.

eyes to the sin of covetousness, but was totally unable to keep him from it. On the contrary, he had found by bitter experience that the command not to covet had had the diametrically opposite effect of producing in him 'every kind of covetous desire'.[21] The fault, he still affirmed, did not lie with the commandment, but rather with sin (which he had begun to see as an almost personified force which had 'taken him captive')[22] and with the weakness of his own 'sinful nature'.[23] So the anomalous result was that 'the very commandment that was intended to bring life' had in fact brought him death[24] — until he found the true solution to his problem, first by seeing that he was now, in Christ, no longer a man 'under the law' in the old way, or subject to its condemnation, and secondly by realizing that, as he lived in the Spirit, he would be able increasingly to fulfil the 'righteous requirements' of the law through love.

Both Scripture and life had taught him, moreover, that this was no unique, personal experience — although it is possible that one with his fiery zeal for God felt it more poignantly than less ardent or more tranquil spirits. He had even come to see that, in this respect at least, the Jew was in no better position than the Gentile; for it was not the outward but the inward that counted, and on this level Jews and Gentiles were alike all 'under sin'.[25] No one whatever could be justified or 'declared righteous' in God's sight on the basis of law-keeping; for all, without exception, had sinned, and all continually fell short of the only standard that a holy God must necessarily demand from those who were determined to stand before him on their own merits.[26] The law could indeed open men's eyes and convict them of their sin, which was one of the primary purposes for which it

---

[21] Romans 7:7 and 8.   [22] Romans 7:11 and 23.   [23] Romans 8:3.
[24] Romans 7:10. There are, of course, a variety of views about the interpretation of Romans 7. Cf. the commentaries by C. E. B. Cranfield and E. Käsemann.   [25] Romans 3:9.   [26] Romans 3:20 and 23.

had been given; but, far from saving them from their sin, unregenerate men found that their 'sinful passions' were actually 'aroused by the law'.[27]

No wonder, then, that Paul seems at times to have rejoiced at being saved, delivered, or 'released' from the law in very much the same way in which he did at being set free from sin, Satan, the 'old man' and death. This was not because he wanted God to 'give him up' to go his own way, which he realized was the worst fate that could befall anyone;[28] what he longed for was to become a willing 'slave to righteousness'. But for this there was only one way: to die to one's old self and its masters[29] – Satan, sin, death and the law – and become a new creature.[30] And he came to realize that this was just what the Cross and Resurrection meant, both for him and others; for the Lord who had forgiven us 'all our sins' had also 'cancelled the written code, with its regulations, that was against us' and had won a spectacular victory at the Cross against Satan and all his powers.[31] So now Paul could joyfully proclaim that 'what the law was powerless to do, in that it was weakened by our sinful nature', God had in fact done 'by sending his own Son in the likeness of sinful man to be a sin offering'; for in this way he had 'condemned sin in sinful man, in order that the righteous requirements of the law might be fully met in us, who do not live according to the sinful nature but according to the Spirit'.[32] And I take this last verse primarily to mean what God has himself done for us, in Christ, in regard to the claims of the law, and only in a secondary sense that we are now enabled by the Spirit ourselves to live on a new plane of obedience. So it was Christ who had made all the difference. Saul the Pharisee had, no doubt, regarded the Christians' testimony to a crucified Messsiah as arrant blasphemy in view of the categorical statement in Deuteronomy 21:23 that

---

[27] Romans 3:19 and 7:5. [28] Romans 1:24, 26 and 28. [29] Romans 6:16 ff.
[30] 2 Corinthians 5:17. [31] Colossians 2:13-15. [32] Romans 8:3 f.

'anyone who is hung on a tree is under God's curse'. But the vision he had had on the Damascus road had proved to him conclusively that Jesus, far from being under God's curse, had been exalted to his right hand. So a fundamental change of mind on this matter must, as Professor F. F. Bruce insists, have been one of the earliest elements in Paul's new theology, for

> Sooner rather than later Paul must have reached the conclusion . . . that Jesus submitted to the death of the cross in order to take upon himself the curse which the law pronounced on all who failed to keep it completely (Dt. 27:26). . . . The *form* of this argument was such as Paul was quite familiar with in the rabbinical schools, but no Rabbi had ever formulated the *substance* of this bold argument – that the Messiah should undergo voluntarily the curse denounced upon the breakers of God's law in order to liberate them from that curse. But in this way the doctrine of a crucified Messiah, which had once been such a stone of stumbling to Paul, became the corner-stone of his faith and preaching.[33]

But what had prompted the One who was now his Lord to make such a sublime act of self-sacrifice? The reason why he had come to suffer a shameful and agonizing death, Paul saw, was 'to redeem those under law, that we might receive the full rights of sons';[34] and the motive power behind it all was that 'he loved me, and gave himself for me'.[35] So Paul was determined never for a moment to 'set aside' this grace of God, 'for if righteousness could be gained through the law, Christ died for nothing'.[36] This was why he went so far as to oppose Peter to his face at Antioch,[37] because he had compromised in this matter; why he pressed the Galatians to

---

[33] F. F. Bruce, *Romans* (Tyndale Press, London, 1963), p. 37.
[34] Galatians 4:5.   [35] Galatians 2:20.   [36] Galatians 2:21.
[37] Galatians 2:11.

answer the simple question 'Did you receive the Spirit by observing the law, or by believing what you heard?'[38]; and why he insisted that the law was only put in charge of the Jews (as a sort of attendant) to look after them, as it were, and lead them to Christ and justification by faith.[39] For God's purpose was that 'just as sin reigned in death, so also grace [that is, the free, unmerited love of God] might reign through righteousness to bring eternal life through Jesus Christ our Lord'.[40] This was why, 'at just the right time, when we were still powerless, Christ died for the ungodly'.[41] It would be very rare, the Apostle continues, for anyone to die even for a righteous man. 'But God demonstrates his own love for us in this: While we were still sinners, Christ died for us.'[42] And the sole reason, of course, why the love of the Saviour who died demonstrates 'God's *own* love' was because of the essential unity, in the eternal Godhead, of the Father who sent and the Son who came. On any other basis the whole logic of Paul's argument would be broken. It was God himself who 'was reconciling the world to himself in Christ, not counting men's sins against them'.[43] So how sure and unshakeable our salvation must be − since 'if, when we were God's enemies, we were reconciled to him through the death of his Son, how much more, having been reconciled, shall we be saved through [or, better, 'in'] his life'.[44] Nor is this basic message of the Gospel in any way confined to this particular letter.

Now it is clearly impossible, in the scope of this chapter, to deal with the development, vicissitudes, controversies and divisions in the Christian Church (in the Apostolic, Sub-Apostolic, Patristic, Scholastic, Reformation and other periods) in any way that is remotely adequate or comprehensive. The infant Church was at once faced with a number of

[38] Galatians 3:2.   [39] Galatians 3:24, or 'until Christ came, so that they might be justified by faith'.   [40] Romans 5:21.   [41] Romans 5:6.
[42] Romans 5:8.   [43] 2 Corinthians 5:19.   [44] Romans 5:10.

acute problems. Must Gentiles, when they responded to
Christ as Saviour and Lord, become a new brand of Jewish
proselytes and try to conform to the Mosaic Law? In what
sense, indeed, had Christ 'fulfilled' that Law, and how was
the Church now to regard it? But there were more fundamental questions even than these. In Christology, for
example, it is clear that the resurrection represented the
watershed after which the primitive Church began instinctively to associate Jesus with the Lord God of Israel. It gave
him the title 'Lord', and started to apply to him Old Testament verses which manifestly spoke of Jahweh himself.
Christians now felt free – and even constrained – to worship
their exalted Lord and sometimes to address him directly in
prayer. So what had become of their basic Jewish mono-
theism; and how, precisely, were they to regard the one who
had lived among them for some thirty years? Was he just an
uniquely Spirit-filled man? Was he God himself, in some
man-like theophany? Was he, perhaps, some sort of com-
posite or intermediate being, or God-man? Or was he essentially God, but God revealing himself in a truly human life:
God-in-manhood? I have grappled with some of these questions, and the contemporary debate which revolves around
them, very recently elsewhere[45] – and this is not the place to
renew the discussion. But the Church had also to reckon
with the world in which it lived: with the power of Rome, its
demand for Emperor worship, and waves of savage persecution; with Gnosticism in its ever-varied guises; with
Neoplatonism in both its pagan and its 'Christianized'
forms; with the confident dogmatism of a re-discovered
Aristotelian philosophy, and its concept of a God who was
little more than a monistic abstraction; and with recurrent
manifestations of a mysticism that ran the gamut between a
virtually pantheistic inclusiveness, a rapturous extremism

[45] Cf. *The Mystery of the Incarnation* (Hodder and Stoughton, London,
1978).

which at times passed beyond the bounds of sanity, and a saintliness and devotion which are both attractive and impressive. All I can attempt is to refer to a number of points which are germane to the subject of this book.

Now we have already seen that Jews, Christians and Muslims, particularly in the Scholastic period, trod the *via negativa* virtually together. Thus Maimonides insisted that 'a positive or affirmative description of anything must state its causes and conditions . . . and for this reason it cannot be made of God who is without cause, and unconditional and not contingent'.[46] So Maimonides was forced to accept the *via negativa* and to assert that the divine attributes merely negate imperfections. But this, if pressed to its logical conclusion, 'would mean that ultimately we must despair of any metaphysical knowledge of God at all'.[47] Similarly, St Thomas Aquinas asserted that 'Everything predicated of God signifies not His substance but rather shows forth what He is *not*'. It is true that the Angelic Doctor would 'not allow the purely philosophical *via negativa* to dominate his thought'; yet he repeatedly emphasized that God is 'utterly other' and 'completely transcendent' – in opposition, respectively, to the *tashbīh* and *tajsīm* (anthropomorphism and embodiment) of some Muslims and to similar views among Christians. But the result, as so often, was that the pendulum swung to the other extreme; so, paradoxically enough, while the human intellect was exalted, man's intrinsic dignity as 'made in the image of God' was put in the gravest jeopardy by such statements as 'Perfections in God cannot be expressed . . . by us except either by negation as when we say that God is *eternal* and *infinite*, or by referring Him to other things as when we say that He is First Cause or Supreme Good . . . for *we are only able to grasp, not what God is, but what He is not*'.[48]

46 J. W. Sweetman, *Islam and Christian Theology* (Part II, Vol. 2, Lutterworth Press, London, 1967), p. 208.   [47] *Ibid.*   [48] *Ibid.*, pp. 209, 317, 323, etc.

In point of fact some of the Schoolmen — Jewish, Christian and Muslim alike — became so obsessed by the fear that they might 'prejudice the concept of the absolute independence of God' that they even wondered, at times, whether in ascribing to him the role of Creator they might not be guilty of attributing to him a transition from potentiality to activity.[49] But to this idea Maimonides, Aquinas and al-Ghazzālī were all opposed. St Thomas, for instance, held that the conception that God is 'cause [or creator] by the necessity of His nature does not necessarily involve belief in the eternity of the universe, and that, in the relation between cause and effect, it is not required that there should be contemporaneity of effect and cause'.[50] Starting from the Platonist postulate that 'He was Good and therefore must impart Himself',[51] it is perfectly natural to argue that in the Creation (and also, for the Christian, in the Incarnation) God has acted, not under any form of external coercion, but by the spontaneous outworking of His own character. So could not exactly the same be said of the love which, the New Testament affirms, is the very essence of his nature — whereas it is not so much as mentioned in the eternal qualities of God which Islamic theology constantly enumerates?

It is precisely at this point that the *via negativa* has such a stultifying effect. No better example of this could, perhaps, be found than in the thought of such a towering and singularly enlightened Muslim as al-Ghazzālī, the declared opponent of the metaphysicians, of whom it has been said that he 'heaps negative upon negative in his summary of the essentials of the Ash'arite creed'. Of these only a very abbreviated summary must suffice. Thus he dogmatically affirms that

> Allah is in His essence one, without a partner, unique with no one like Him, eternal and without an

[49] *Ibid.*, p. 303.   [50] *Ibid.*, p. 304.   [51] *Ibid.*, p. 307.

opposite, sole and without a peer. He does not resemble any object of existence and no object of existence resembles Him, He is like nothing and nothing is like Him. He is distinct from His creation in His qualities. He transcends change and alteration. He has created the creatures and their acts and has apportioned their provisions and their deaths. He is the willer of all that comes to be, the one who sets in order all temporal events. Nothing occurs in His kingship and kingdom, little or much, small or great, good or ill, profitable or harmful, faith or unbelief, familiarity or ignorance, success or failure, increase or decrease, obedience or disobedience, except by His decree (*qaḍā'*) and power (*qadar*), His wisdom and will (*mashī'a*). What He has willed has come to be and what He has not willed has not come to be. No one can refuse His command and no one can delay His decree and the creature has no refuge from his sin except by Allah's *tawfīq* (the assistance afforded by Allah) and His mercy and has no power to be obedient except by His wish. Hence God has these attributes. He is living, knowing, powerful, willing, hearing, seeing, speaking,[52] by life, power, knowledge, will, hearing, sight and speech and not simply by essence.[53]

Now, much of this is, of course, profoundly true. But if there is really this complete and utter dissimilarity between the Creator and all his creatures, then in what possible sense can men and women be said to have been created 'in his image and after his likeness'? Again, if everything (including faith and unbelief, obedience and disobedience) not only depends on his permissive will but happens by his direct decree and volitional will or desire, then what becomes of the moral responsibility of men and women? Surely, too, it is

---

[52] These are the seven attributes of God to which many references have been made.   [53] *Ibid.* Extracts from pp. 21-24.

very strange that the list of the seven eternal attributes of God gives no place whatever to that love for his creatures which Christians believe to be the very heart of his Being, and to which Muslims themselves give at least verbal expression in the beautiful names they attribute to him? Again, while Christians would agree that the reason for the creation was not that God stood in need of it (for his eternal love could be, and indeed was, expressed *within* the triune Godhead before anyone or anything else existed), yet surely it was, in part at least, occasioned by the fact that he had 'set his love upon the sons of men' and had purposed to 'bring many sons to glory'? It would, no doubt, be going too far to follow Palgrave's austere summary of the Muslim view of God:

> Immeasurably and eternally exalted above and dis-similar from all creatures . . . sterile in His inaccessible height, neither loving nor enjoying aught save His own and self-measured decree, without son, companion and counsellor, He is no less barren of Himself than for His creatures.[54]

— since there are many Muslims who would indignantly repudiate this statement. But even in the teaching of Aquinas God is utterly immutable as well as impassible, for 'nothing in God begins anew'.[55] So here there is a considerable area of agreement between Jewish, Christian and Muslim Scholastics which is in each case, I think, derived from the Aristotelian philosophy which was at this time common to them all and largely expressed in a whole series of negatives. 'We cannot know God and yet we can have an idea of God so as to be able to negate of Him all that is opposed to that idea',[56] the *Summa Theologica* (I, q. 3) affirms. And 'in this context those words of Aquinas', Sweet-man justly remarks, 'are echoed by Muslim and Christian

[54] *Central and Eastern Arabia*, Vol. 1, p. 365 — quoted by Sweetman, *op. cit.*, p. 321.   [55] Sweetman, *op. cit.*, p. 324.   [56] *Op. cit.*, p. 326.

alike, and even the mystics favour the *via negativa*[57] — in spite of their attachment to *kashf*, or the direct revelation of God to the human heart. Indeed, the importance of correct theology was emphasized in both Christendom and Islam to the point where 'debates on heresy assumed the character of judicial enquiries' and 'religion came to be thought of and spoken of as *"lex"*.'[58] So the conclusion seems obvious: that theism, *per se*, is not enough. 'The achievement of great thinkers resulting in a comparable and intelligible exposition or deep debate on metaphysical questions cannot do justice to a theological encounter in which, for the Christian, Jesus Christ . . . stands as the central figure.'[59] Aristotelian Scholasticism is probably kinder to a unitarian system than to an incarnational religion like Christianity, Sweetman observes; but when we turn either to the Bible or the Qur'ān it becomes obvious that *neither* can confine God to remote history, 'so that He becomes a lifeless, abstract symbol of an outlived past'.[60] The philosophical conclusion that 'God is free from passions and is not affected by any emotion of joy and sorrow', and that 'strictly speaking, God neither loves nor hates anybody',[61] is a desperately sterile position to maintain.

So, although Christians and Muslims have trod the *via negativa* a long way together, there is a point at which they must, of necessity, part company. It would not be true to say that this is where the so-called *via positiva* begins, for some Muslim mystics have travelled a considerable distance along that road too in at least partial company with their counterparts in the Christian tradition. After all, Neoplatonism — as Professor D. B. Macdonald has roundly asserted — is 'the foundation of the philosophy of Islam'.[62] This probably reached scholars like al-Fārābi through the works of

[57] *Ibid.*   [58] *Ibid*, p. 328.   [59] *Op. cit.*, p. 329.   [60] *Ibid.*, p. 331.
[61] Spinoza, *Ethics*, I, 17, quoted by Sweetman, *ibid.*, p. 327.
[62] *Muslim Theology, Jurisprudence and Constitutional Theory*, pp. 180 f.

Porphyry, the biographer and literary executor of Plotinus; and early Christian philosophy and mysticism was largely based on a somewhat uneasy reconciliation between Biblical revelation and Neoplatonic speculation. This is true even of St Augustine. It was, moreover, chiefly through Christian mystics – and especially through Dionysius the Pseudo-Areopagite – that Neoplatonism had such a profound influence on later Muslim Ṣūfīs; and this same author's writings were approved by Gregory the Great and the Lateran Council of 649, for example. Muslims did not, of course, accept his attempted synthesis between Christian faith and Neoplatonic thought; but one of his works, which describes the ascent of the human soul towards God through the purgative, the illuminative and the unitive stages, had a widespread influence on both Christian and Muslim mystics. For the Ṣūfīs, it was only in ecstasy that man could come to a direct and personal knowledge of God;[63] and in both the Jewish and Christian traditions visions, dreams, trances and ecstatic rapture have certainly played their part. We may recall, as examples, Isaiah's vision of 'the Lord, seated on a throne, high and exalted', as recorded in Isaiah 6; or the incident to which Paul makes a very guarded reference in 2 Corinthians 12:1-5, when he was 'caught up to the third heaven' and 'heard inexpressible things, things that man is not permitted to tell'.

In general, it seems that there are two main types of mysticism. One of these is essentially introvertive, in which the mystic

> by turning inwards on his own consciousness and experience, and by stressing the necessity for discarding from his mind all visual or concrete images, comes to realize in a peculiarly coercive way his essential oneness with ultimate reality.

[63] *Ibid.*, pp. 181 f.

The other, which may be termed extrovertive, is 'closely akin to the experience of the poet and the prophet',[64] and is often linked with some objective experience or circumstance – or with what the early Christian Fathers called the 'mystery'. Another classification, which is favoured by Professor R. C. Zaehner, is into nature mystics, monistic mystics and theistic mystics.[65] Evelyn Underhill has herself warned us, moreover, that even in theistic or specifically Christian mysticism

> We must not be afraid to admit that some of the experiences, actions and conceptions which we find among the mystics were excessive and distorted; that they were sometimes affected by mistaken views both of divine and human nature, or attributed spiritual value to emotion of a lower kind. . . . A mystic is not necessarily a perfect human being [sic]; and the imperfections and crudities of his character or outlook may influence and mingle with his mysticism.[66]

It is exceedingly difficult, in point of fact, to draw any firm line between mystical visions and experiences which are basically from God – even if subject, to some extent, to limitations imposed by the temperament, environment or background of the individuals concerned – and what is purely emotional, imaginative, psychological, Satanic or merely the result of techniques designed to induce mystical consciousness, for it is obvious that to attain such states men have often

> willingly submitted themselves to elaborate ascetic procedures. . . . They have practised fasting, flagellation, and sensory deprivation, and, in so doing, may have

[64] E. J. Tinsley, article on 'Mysticism' in *A Dictionary of Christian Theology*, (ed. Alan Richardson, SCM Press, 1969), p. 226.
[65] *Mysticism, Sacred and Profane* (OUP, 1957), pp. 28 ff., 153 ff.
[66] *The Mystics of the Church* (James Clarke & Co., Cambridge, 1975), p. 16.

attained to states of heightened mystical consciousness, but also have succeeded in altering their body chemistry. Recent physiological investigations . . . tend to confirm the notion that provoked alterations in body chemistry and body rhythm are in no small way responsible for the dramatic changes in consciousness attendant upon these practices.[67]

In addition, there is overwhelming evidence that drugs of various sorts have been used for this purpose for centuries, and are in widespread demand today.[68]

But the basic point at which the Christian must, of necessity, part company with all others is, of course, in regard to the Incarnation — as we have already noted in passing. It is in this context that Evelyn Underhill justly remarks:

> Christianity is unique among the world's great religions in this: that its Founder is to His closest followers not merely a prophet, pattern of conduct, or Divine figure revealed in the historic past, but the object here and now of an experienced communion of the most vivid kind. Christians claim that this communion has continued unimpaired for nineteen hundred years, and is the true source of the Church's undying energy. Those persons who have — in continuous succession since the first Easter — most vividly experienced this, have been the means of making the Church's loyalty to her Master a living thing. These people are properly to be called mystics; for believers in the Incarnation must, with the Fourth Evangelist, regard their apprehension as an apprehension of God in Christ.[69]

But it remains true that

[67] R. E. L. Masters and Jean Houston, *The Varieties of Psychedelic Experience* (Hoit, Rinehart and Winston, New York, 1966), pp. 248 f. [68] Cf. my *Christianity and Comparative Religion* (Tyndale Press, London, 1970), pp. 20 ff.   [69] *Op. cit.*, p. 24.

There are, of course, two distinct but complementary currents in Christian feeling and worship. One is directed towards God, the Eternal and Infinite Spirit; the other towards His incarnate revelation in Jesus Christ. These two strains are reflected in Christian mystical experience. On the one hand, we have a group of mystics of whom St Augustine and St Catherine of Genoa are supreme types, whose dominant spiritual apprehension is of the absolute Being of God, and of the soul's union with Him. In technical language, they are 'theocentric'. God is realized by them under more or less impersonal symbols, and especially as Light and Love. . . . Mystics of this temperament often show close correspondence with the experience of other great lovers of God, outside the Christian fold. This should not surprise us; for since God is one, and 'is not far from any one of us', there must be a common element in our limited human apprehension of Him.[70]

On the other hand, the inner life of many of the most ardent Christian mystics is controlled by their sense of a direct personal communion with our Lord; there are 'Christocentric', and can say with Walter Hinton that for them 'God, grace and Jesus are all one'. Within that consciousness of God as the eternal and abiding Reality, which is perhaps *the* mystical sense, this type of religious experience apprehends the intimate presence here and now of a personal Love, identified by them with the Risen and Exalted Christ and accepted as Master, Companion and Helper of the soul. . . .[71]

In the individual, Evelyn Underhill writes, one or other of these "streams of feeling", the theocentric and the Christo-

---

[70] This point is discussed, briefly, below.   [71] *Op. cit.*, pp. 23-25.

centric, inevitably tends to predominate. But some of the greatest Christian mystics (such as St Paul, Jacopone da Todi, Julian of Norwich, St Teresa and Ruysbroeck, she suggests) have 'included in their sweep both the historical and the unchanging manifestations of the Divine Life'. And I suppose that this means that they have come to see 'the light of the knowledge of the glory of God in the face of Jesus Christ',[72] or — to put it in other words — that the Lord Jesus has done what he came to do: namely, bring them to God.[73]

Is it possible, then, to suggest any tests as to what is, and what is not, of divine origin? The answer must, I think, be 'Yes' — but only with humility and caution, for it seems to me impossible to go to either of two extremes: to accept *all* alleged mystical experiences as genuinely from God, which is manifestly not true; or to dismiss as spurious every such experience which is not consciously mediated by the incarnate Lord. Surely the God who could and did reveal himself to the Old Testament saints can still speak directly — or, indeed, through 'the true light that gives light to every man' — to those who truly seek him? We need to remember the many promises there are in the Bible that those who really seek God will find him.[74] It is noteworthy, too, that one of the ways in which mystics most commonly seek after God is by trying to plumb the depths of their own hearts; and it is in this context that William Temple wrote:

> Because man is made in the image of God, the attempt to find God through penetrating to the inmost recesses of the self leads in men of all times and races to a similar experience. God truly is the spring of life in our souls; so to seek that spring is to seek Him; and to find it would be to find Him.

But he immediately adds these words of very salutary warning:

[72] 2 Corinthians 4:6.   [73] Cf. 1 Peter 3:18. Cf. Matthew 11:27.
[74] Cf., *inter alia*, Proverbs 8:17; Luke 11:9; Lamentations 3:25; Acts 17:27; and Hebrews 11:6.

But this can never quite happen. The image of God in man is defaced by sin, that is by self-will. The mind which seeks to reach that image is distorted by sin, and moulded both for good and evil by tradition. The *via negativa* of the mystics cannot be perfectly followed. To rely on a supposedly direct communion with God in detachment from all external aids is to expose the soul to suggestions arising from its distortion as well as to those arising from the God whom it would apprehend. Mediation there must be; imagery there must be. If we do not deliberately avail ourselves of the true Mediator, the 'express image' (Hebrews 1:3), we shall be at the mercy of some unworthy medium and of a distorted image. If we are learning to see God in Christ, let us by all means steep our minds in that revelation, and repose in God so made known to us with complete immediacy of surrender and trust. But let us be sure that the knowledge of God on which we rely is that which reaches us through Jesus, the Word of God made flesh.[75]

This is invaluable advice for the Christian. But what about all those who lived before Christ, or those who, even today, have never had any real opportunity to get to know him? What can we say about them? And what tests would be applicable (should anyone be in a position to apply them) to the mystical experiences they may claim?

One such test which has already emerged in this chapter is a genuine desire to find God and know him as he really is. But another — which is, to me at least, almost equally important — is to have a God-given sense of sin or unworthiness. For what we need so badly is not only an objective revelation of God, but a subjective attitude of heart which

[75] *Readings in St John's Gospel* (First Series, Macmillan & Co., London, 1942), pp. 92 f.

will enable us to apprehend it. There can be no doubt, moreover, that many mystics have in some sense realized this, as can be seen from the place they have habitually given (and presumably still give) to the purgative stage in the mystic path. But there is an essential difference between asceticism, with all that commonly accompanies it in the search for purgation, on the one hand, and a heart-felt cry for divine forgiveness, on the other; for, whereas the purgative stage in a mystic's initiation may be largely a matter of self-effort and human achievement, the plea for forgiveness turns the penitent's eyes away from himself to the love and undeserved mercy of the God he seeks. To take an example from Muslim mystics, we are told that Rābi'a al-Addawiyya, the woman saint who died in 135 AH, not only put a major emphasis on disinterested love in all her teaching, but was so given to weeping that the place of her devotions was like a bog from her many tears. One of her sayings quoted by al-Sha'rānī, moreover, is that 'our seeking of forgiveness itself needs a seeking of forgiveness'. Again, Ibrāhim ibn Adham, who died in the year 161 AH, is said often to have prayed: 'O God, uplift me from the shame of disobedience to the glory of submission to Thee' – a prayer which at least suggests what seems to me the third essential: a self-abandonment to the mercy of God. If these three criteria are fulfilled – a genuine search after God, a heart-felt plea for forgiveness, and a self-abandonment to God's mercy (all of which must, surely, be evidence of the Holy Spirit's inward working) – I cannot but believe that the seeking soul will either hear and receive the message of forgiveness and peace in this life, like Cornelius, or will wake up, as it were, on the other side of the grave to worship the Saviour in whom he found this mercy without understanding how.[76]

[76] I have discussed this question much more fully in *Christianity and Comparative Religion*.

But we are concerned in this chapter primarily with Christians, who base their faith in and knowledge of God not on any mystical experiences of their own but on the Incarnation, Passion and Resurrection of their Lord. It was there that God spoke decisively to men and women – and still speaks to them – from the midst of human experience, assuring them of his love, forgiveness and abiding presence. It is significant, in this context, that while Paul refused to 'boast' of the ecstatic experience to which, as we have seen, he made such a reticent reference in 2 Corinthians 12, he was perfectly willing to boast of his 'weaknesses', and of the fact that it was in them that the power of the living Christ was most perfectly displayed. Somewhat similarly, Evelyn Underhill remarks that:

> Ecstatic phenomena were almost taken for granted in the Early Church; and St Paul's distinction as a mystic lies not in their possession, but in the detachment with which he regarded them. Thus . . . when he wrote his first letter to the Corinthians, he acknowledged his continued possession of the much-prized 'gift of tongues'; those outbursts of ecstatic but unintelligible speech common in times of religious excitement. But his attitude towards such external 'manifestations of the Spirit' is marked by a cool common sense which must amaze us when we consider the period in which he wrote, the universal respect for the marvellous, and the circumstances of his own conversion. His rule was simple. He discounts any 'gifts' and experiences which do not help other souls. The mystical communion of his soul with Christ must not be a matter of personal enjoyment: it must support and not supplant the apostolic career.[77]

For the Christian, then, the centre and core of faith is not

[77] *Op. cit.*, pp. 44 f.

some new and personal revelation, but an ever-closer identification with the supreme revelation of God which has been
given once for all in history. When, moreover, anyone
claims to have had a mystical or ecstatic experience, the acid
test is severely practical – for in this, too, 'by their *fruits* you
will recognize them'.[78] Our task is to witness to Christ, and
our supreme goal is that he 'may dwell in our hearts by faith'
and that we may 'know the love of Christ which surpasses
knowledge'.[79]

Does this mean, then, that love is so absolutely central in
the Christian life that it should constitute our only
'absolute', and that law can be reduced to no more than a
mere form of 'guidelines' as to how love should normally be
expressed – as some of the devotees of 'Situation Ethics' so
constantly insist? In a perfect world this might, indeed, be
so, for the New Testament certainly teaches that 'love is the
fulfilment of the law'.[80] But we do not live in a perfect world;
so how are ignorant, fallen human beings always to know
what the highest love demands – not only in terms of themselves, when under deep emotional pressure, nor even for
one other person who may be primarily concerned, but for
third parties too, and even society as a whole? We all know
that hard cases make bad law, and that bad law – in its
turn – adversely affects the whole community. As William
Temple once remarked, if one has to decide the problem of
what wages should rightfully be paid for this job or that, the
criterion must be justice rather than love; and the slick reply
that justice is only another term for 'distributive love'
stretches the latter word so far as almost to evacuate it of
meaning. This is why God our Creator has given us laws of
abiding validity which must not be down-graded to mere
guidelines. But the fact remains that there are occasions, in
this very imperfect world, when two of these laws or

[78] Matthew 7:20.   [79] Ephesians 3:17-19.   [80] Romans 13:10.

principles of abiding validity come into headlong collision. In such cases the only solution for the Christian is to choose (often in agony of spirit) the lesser of two evils — conscious, indeed, that what he is doing is not *intrinsically* right (since it is contrary to a moral command of abiding validity), yet driven to the conclusion that, in the particular circumstances, he can make no other choice. This is not an example of 'Situation Ethics', as its advocates expound it, but of what has aptly been termed 'Principled Ethics'. Nor is it a case of love triumphing over law, but rather of love acting as arbiter between two laws one of which must, in the circumstances, give way to the other.

In point of fact, law and love must of necessity always go together, for we are told that God himself is both 'light' and 'love'[81] — and in this context the term 'light' cannot primarily mean illumination but, rather, transparent holiness and moral purity, in which 'there is no darkness at all'. It is, moreover, the ultimate objective of God's 'perfect law of liberty' (that is, a way of life perfectly fitted to our nature and situation[82] which liberates us from the bondage into which we so easily slip) that we should 'walk in the light, as he is in the light'.[83] That is why one of the basic New Testament definitions of sin is 'lawlessness',[84] why sins of omission are regarded as just as heinous as sins of commission (as we see from the judgement of the sheep and the goats in Matthew 25:31 ff., with its haunting yet remorseless indictment: 'whatever you did *not* do for one of the least of these, you did not do for me'), and why our love for God is defined not in terms of sentimental piety or even doctrinal correctness, but simply as 'to obey his commands'.[85] But, while we certainly have to 'work out [our] own salvation with fear and

[81] 1 John 1:5 and 4:6(b).   [82] Cf. J. A. Motyer, *Studies in St James* (New Mildmay Press, London, 1968), p. 22.   [83] 1 John 1:6 f.
[84] 1 John 3:4. Cf. 2 Thessalonians 2:3-9.   [85] 1 John 5:3.

trembling'[86] and 'make every effort'[87] to add one Christian virtue to another, there is ultimately only one way in which we can learn to love. John states this in its shortest form, and with sublime simplicity, when he says 'We love because he first loved us'.[88] He does not say (with the AV) that this is why we love *him*, although this is true; what he says is that this is why we know what love really means. Putting it in another way, Paul tells us that 'God has poured out his love into our hearts by the Holy Spirit, whom he has given us'[89] – and that, because of this, we 'who with unveiled faces . . . contemplate [or reflect] the Lord's glory, are being transformed into his likeness'.[90] All the same, we need the grace of God's forgiveness right to the end of the road, for James will not let us forget that 'whoever keeps the whole law, and yet stumbles at just one point, is guilty of breaking all of it'.[91] This does not, of course, mean that a man who tells a lie is guilty of murder; but it does mean that he is a law-breaker, and stands condemned as such.

But we are concerned not with our love for God, but with his matchless love for us, although these verses all testify, indirectly but unmistakeably, to the love of God himself. Similarly, a mystic's love for God (with at least the implication of some divine initiative or response), together with a law – itself based on the character of the Law-giver – which commands us to love, both bear their indirect but inescapable witness to the love he has for his creatures. But I am reminded that Henry Drummond, in his moving address on 'The Greatest Thing in the World', after quoting Paul's words in 1 Corinthians 13:13

> And now these three remain: faith, hope and love. But the greatest of these is love

pointed out that, while the Apostle said that prophecies will

---

[86] Philippians 2:12.   [87] 2 Peter 1:5.   [88] 1 John 4:19.   [89] Romans 5:5.
[90] 2 Corinthians 3:18.   [91] James 2:10.

cease, that tongues will be stilled and that knowledge will pass away, he did not commit himself to the commonly held view that faith and hope will also 'pass away' – faith into sight and hope into fruition. What he did say is that 'What is certain is that Love must last', for 'God, the Eternal God, is Love'. He did not mention Law at all in this context; but I am tempted to think that, had he lived in the Communist era, he might have sympathized with their one-time belief that law (like the State) would eventually 'wither away' – because its work had been done, and we were all 'made perfect in love'.[92] But would he? For law, to Henry Drummond, meant the truth – the way things are – and that, too, is 'eternal'. So I fancy that his attitude would have been that the 'stern' side even of God's law, in its necessary function of restraining and punishing evil (in the sense, for example, that

> the law is made not for good men but for lawbreakers and rebels, the ungodly and sinful, the unholy and ir-religious; for those who kill their fathers or mothers, for murderers, for adulterers and perverts, for slave traders and liars and perjurers – and for whatever else is contrary to the sound doctrine that conforms to the glorious gospel of the blessed God, which he entrusted to me'[93])

would have been left behind, indeed, when love had come into its own; but that in essence the Law of God and the Love of God would ever remain in perfect harmony, as complementary characteristics of the God who is – eternally and in his very nature – light, truth and love.

But, however that may be, the inevitable interconnection between God's love and ours – and, still more, the pre-eminent role played by the Incarnation in proving the love of God in a way that leaves the *via negativa* far behind – is

[92] 1 John 4:18.   [93] 1 Timothy 1:9 ff.

shown in a passage like this:

> love comes from God. Everyone who loves has been
> born of God and knows God. Whoever does not love
> does not know God, because God is love. This is how
> God showed his love among us: He sent his one and
> only Son into the world that we might live through
> him. This is love: not that we loved God, but that he
> loved us and sent his Son as an atoning sacrifice for our
> sins. . . . No one has ever seen God; but if we love each
> other, God lives in us and his love is made complete in
> us.[94]

---

[94]1 John 4:7.

CHAPTER 5

The Law of God and the Love of God: The Problem of Suffering and Evil

It is virtually impossible to consider either the Law of God or the Love of God without reflecting, with deep perplexity, about some of the phenomena of human life which we encounter continually, whether in our own experience or that of our relatives, friends or confidants: sin, suffering, calamity and evil in all its forms, whether material or moral. How is it that this dark side of life, which obtrudes itself so constantly (both in the media and in a more personal way), can co-exist with the Law — and, still less, with the Love — of a God who is said to be both omnipotent and loving? No man, whatever his religion, can ignore this problem, or fail to make some sort of response to its challenge. But while the sufferings and calamities of some may be so acute that they have little time for abstract thought about their theological implications, there are others to whom the theoretical and spiritual problems involved may be even more baffling than their practical and material manifestations.[1]

To the simple minded polytheist the immediate problem is, I suppose, basically practical. For him the world is

---

[1] For a detailed and scholarly treatment of this whole subject, cf. John Bowker, *Problems of Suffering in Religions of the World* (CUP, 1970).

occupied, or even dominated, by a variety of gods and spirits, some primarily beneficent but most of them potentially malignant – corresponding, fairly closely, with his experience of purely natural phenomena, with what he has learnt to expect from his contemporaries and with the stories he has heard from his ancestors. The vital thing, then, is for him to keep on good terms with those gods or spirits with whom he is in any sort of relationship, and to do all he can to ward off the evil which those whom he has chanced to offend, or who are liable to be manipulated by his enemies, may wish to bring upon his head. In point of fact almost all polytheists have at least a background belief in a Creator God, however habitually they ignore him in practice and concern themselves primarily with other – more immanent and malignant – spirits. So they, too, *may* sometimes ask themselves why this Creator God ever brought such a variety of spirits into being; but I suspect that normally they simply accept the fact that he did – which, again, fits in with their day to day experience of the phenomena of Nature and the diversity of friendly or hostile tribes, and kind or cruel individuals.

Similarly, I doubt whether the pantheist concerns himself greatly, in any theoretical way, with the problem of evil – however intimately he may be troubled by some of its manifestations in his own experience. To him all Nature – whether beneficent or cruel, tranquil or stormy – is part of the deity; and he is not so much concerned with the abstract problem of why nature is so strangely variegated as with the stark realities of life, in all its vicissitudes, as it actually is. And to the convinced Dualist the theoretical problem must be even less acute. Thus, whatever Zarathushtra, the founder of Zoroastrianism, himself believed and taught, orthodox Zoroastrians of the Sassanian and early Muslim periods had embraced a creed which was starkly dualistic, and which taught that there are two first principles, one the Creator and the other the Destroyer. The Creator is Ohrmazd[2] who is all goodness and all light; and the Destroyer is the accursed Ahriman[3] who is all wickedness and full of death, a liar and a deceiver.

These two principles, the one up on high in the light and the other down below in the darkness, were separated by the 'Void'; but Ohrmazd was always conscious that Ahriman would attack him if he knew of his existence. So he 'created the spiritual and material worlds as a means of self protection'. Thus, at one stroke, as Professor R. C. Zaehner puts it, 'classical' Zoroastrian dualism

> not only solved those two hoary mysteries – the origin of evil and the reason for creation – it drained them of all their mysteriousness. If evil is a separate principle, then its origin is no mystery. Creation too ceases to be a mysterious overflowing of the Godhead and becomes simply the means by which God protects himself from his eternal enemy: God creates because, out of pure self-interest, he has to. Moreover, there is a certain poetic justice in the whole affair; for the Evil One, being by nature chaotic and stupid, is instrumental in destroying himself. He invades the world and brings death, disease and sin into it, but, although his capacity for hurting God's creatures is enormous, the inner compulsion that drives him to his own destruction is stronger still.[4]

So, even in this form of Zoroastrianism, the explicit dualism of two co-eternal principles, one wholly good and the other wholly evil, is qualified, in the last analysis, by the belief

[2] Called Ahura Mazdāh (the 'Wise Lord') at an earlier stage.
[3] Previously known as Angra Mainyu or the Druj (the 'Lie').
[4] R. C. Zaehner, 'Zoroastrianism', in *The Concise Encyclopedia of Living Faiths*, pp. 210 f.

that the good is destined ultimately to prevail.[5]

It is when one turns to Hinduism and Buddhism that things become much more complex. This is partly because of the vast variety of beliefs that are loosely grouped under the exceedingly expansive umbrella of 'Hinduism', and the wide divergence which has developed between the Theravāda and Mahāyāna branches of Buddhism (to say nothing of several more recent sects); and partly because of the intellectual complexity and philosophical profundity of much Hindu and Buddhist thought. In a previous chapter, for example, we have noted some of the basic differences between the philosophies of Śankara and the Advaita-Vedānta, on the one hand, and the Sāṁkhya-Yoga, on the other. Yet the starting point of both is the same: the *experience* of the immortality of the soul. But this emphatically does *not* mean the endless prolongation of life as we know it. On the contrary, this is the great evil from which liberation, or *moksha*, must be sought. But how, precisely, is *moksha* to be defined? The monistic answer in the *Māndūkya* Upanishad is that this state is 'unthinkable' and 'cannot be designated'. It *'causes the phenomenal world to cease*; it is tranquil and mild, devoid of duality'.[6] But another answer, in one of the later Upanishads, is that in *moksha*

> the soul severs its links with matter and therefore knows neither pleasure nor pain, it soars up to the highest light where, no longer merely serene, it becomes serenity (*samprasāda*) itself; but this is a personal serenity which preserves the soul's individual form (*svena svena rūpena*). 'He is the highest person (*uttama purusha*). There he goes around laughing, playing, enjoying himself with women or chariots or friends, remembering nothing of this body which was appended to him.[7]

[5] Cf. E. O. James, *Christianity and Other Religions*, p. 61 etc. Cf. also my *Christianity and Comparative Religion*, p. 81, etc.   [6] Zaehner, Hinduism, p. 75.   [7] *Ibid.*

This view of *moksha*, which 'asserts not only survival in an extra-temporal state but also the survival of personal relationships', is clearly at variance both with the monism of Śankara and the dualism of the Sāṁkhya-Yoga philosophy, and does not seem to have exercised any very deep or lasting influence. Instead, in Zaehner's words,

> the purely monistic view of *moksha* as the complete isolation of the eternal from the temporal was long to hold the day. But in the case of the Advaita the 'eternal' was not simply the eternal essence of one single soul as it was in the Sāṁkhya-Yoga, but Absolute Being or, in Western terminology, the impassible Godhead behind the Creator God. For in Śankara's opinion there was only one reality, Brahman. . . . The Creator God who is so frequently mentioned in the Upanishads as being both the efficient and the material cause of the universe, cannot be wholly identical with Brahman because he is the source and cause of multiplicity. . . .[8]

In the Sāṁkhya-Yoga philosophy, on the other hand, the basic reason why it does not admit any identity between the individual soul and a Supreme Soul is that it denies the existence of the latter and does not really believe in any deity at all.[9] To both schools of thought, however, it is clear that *moksha* does not mean deliverance from sin or moral guilt, but a happy liberation from the *samsāric* world, with all its suffering and frustration.

This suffering, however, can scarcely be said to represent any *theological* problem to those who are not theists. To them *karma* is the eternal law or principle whereby the past *must* influence the present, and the present the future. In this chain of cause and effect no third party can effectively intervene – a consideration which goes far to explain what often seems to be callousness or indifference to the sufferings

---

[8] *Ibid.*   [9] Cf. Zaehner, *op. cit.*, p. 70.

of others. How the Advaita and the Sāṁkhya solve the *philosophical* problem of why illusion (*māyā*) and Nature (*prakṛti*) take the form, and play the roles, that they each, respectively, believe them to do, is a question that does not concern us in this context. Even to *bhakti* theists, however, the doctrine of *karma* seems to provide a key to many of the mysteries inherent in the inequalities of life and the sufferings of the apparently innocent. Suffering is an inescapable experience on the weary road to *moksha* (and, as such, can be regarded as part of the divine law); and the love of God can, perhaps, be chiefly discerned in the grace that may shorten this road and thus hasten final deliverance.

Buddhism and Jainism, both of which represent deviations from Hindu thought, take an even more pessimistic view of the *saṁsāric* world. Thus Professor A. L. Basham writes that Jainism has always maintained, as its fundamental doctrine, that 'the phenomenal individual consists of a soul closely enmeshed in matter', and that 'salvation is to be found by freeing the soul from matter, so that the former may enjoy omniscient self-sufficient bliss for all eternity'. Meanwhile, 'the universe is a place of utter misery and sorrow and its few moments of happiness in no way compensate for the essential horror of existence'. If a man desires salvation he must, therefore,

> subject himself to rigorous hardship and pain to get rid of *karma* already acquired, and act with the utmost circumspection lest he acquire new *karma* in serious quantities. Even the unintentional killing of an ant may have very grave consequences for the soul, and injury with deliberate intention is far more serious than injury through carelessness. Directly or indirectly everyone must do some injury, at least to the lower forms of life in the Jain hierarchy of being, but all Jain ethics are directed towards the one aim of doing as

little injury as possible. No other Indian sect has carried the doctrine of *ahiṁsā* (non-violence) to such extremes.[10]

The Buddhist's attitude to this *saṁsāric* world is almost equally pessimistic.[11] At the very centre of Gautama's 'Enlightenment', as we have already seen,[12] was the overwhelming conviction that sentient existence is, by its very nature, characterized by suffering, which is the direct result of the desire to exist, to possess, to 'become'. The only way to escape from, or to cure, suffering is, therefore, to eliminate any such craving, whatever form it may take – or, as Bishop Stephen Neill puts it:[13]

> How is the problem of suffering to be dealt with? Buddhism adopts the most radical of all solutions: abolish the entity, and therewith we shall abolish the sufferer; abolish the ego, which believes that it suffers, and there will no longer be anything that can suffer. This was the great enlightenment that came to the Buddha under the Bo-tree.

The elimination of the self is the heart and centre of all Buddhist philosophy. What we apprehend as human existence belongs to the realm of *anicca*, the impermanent and perpetually changing, in which there is no abiding reality. Such a realm is necessarily *an-atta*, 'without soul'; there can be no place in it for a permanent centre of human consciousness. Man is not a unity; he is simply the coalescence of five *khandhā*[14]

[10] A. L. Basham, 'Jainism', in *The Concise Encyclopedia of Living Faiths*, pp. 257 ff. But, it may be added, the Buddhist comes little behind the Jain in regard to *ahiṁsā*.   [11] *Pace* Christmas Humphreys, *op. cit.*, p. 83.   [12] Cf. pp. 27, 30 above.   [13] *Christian Faith and Other Faiths* (OUP, London, 1961), pp. 107 ff.   [14] The first of these is *rūpa*, which means the body or material form, while the other four are collectively termed *nāma*, or the non-material parts of a 'being' – 'feeling, perception, the volitional activities or habitual tendencies, and consciousness'. (Cf. I. B. Horner, 'Buddhism: the Theravāda', in *The Concise Encyclopedia of Living Faiths*, p. 280.)

(the word is frequently translated 'aggregates') which happen to come together. . . .

Modern psychology in the West has had difficulty in determining what, if anything, it means by the word *psyche*; on the whole, however, it has held that there is some centre of ideation, some ego, by which all the shifting gleams of experience are held together in some kind of unity. Buddhism cuts the Gordian knot of the problem by radically denying the existence of any such unifying centre. Precisely this is the meaning of the term *an-atta*, without soul.

In the Theravāda form of Buddhism it is only man who can 'free himself from the wheel of *samsāra* or that of the process of becoming. . . . He must win his freedom by dispelling ignorance and darkness and arousing knowledge and light. And he must do it by himself'. Buddhas can, indeed, point the way, but then man must 'swelter at the task'.[15] There is no God to whom he can appeal for help, and Gautama's aid is limited to the *Dharma* or Teaching that he has bequeathed. Man must work out his own salvation. The Theravādin has been born into this world with an entail of *karma* from previous existences, whether as a man, a *deva*[16] or an animal. This *karma* 'may be regarded as an absolutely just but impersonal cosmic operation according to which the fruits or effects ripening of a volitional act or deed of body, speech or thought are suited to that act'.[17] But it must be understood that in Buddhism, in contrast to Hinduism,

> deeds do not necessarily stay and rest with the doer of them. *Karma* passes on, and though in a new birth the doer is not substantially the same as he was in a preceding one nor totally different, there yet has been

[15] I. B. Horner, *op. cit.*, p. 276.   [16] The word comes from the root which means 'to shine'. Devas as beings in other worlds are in certain respects above the human level. But they are *not* gods, angels, or 'celestial beings', (cf. *op. cit.*, p. 292).   [17] *Ibid.*, p. 275.

no discontinuity between the process of dying and that of being born again. Consciousness is a stream and the consciousness there was at the time of death flows on and into the re-birth-consciousness, without interruption.[18]

The Teaching on this subject, which is unique to Buddhism, is termed 'dependent origination'; and may be somewhat elucidated in the statement that

> since there is no 'being' that passes from one 'habitation' to another, it is not precisely 'I' or 'the man so-and-so' that fares on and circles on in *samsāra* or reaps the harvest of good or evil that 'I' or 'he' has sown in some anterior habitation. 'I', 'he', 'being' are words used only in common parlance but in no ultimate sense. Even the Buddhas use these words, however, but are not misled by them.[19]

But, however this may be, man must struggle to get free — free from 'the ignorance that is the fundamental cause of misery and suffering in life after life'; free from untamed grasping after anything in the world; 'free from the taints and defilements of the mind. . . .'[20] The way of escape is not by extreme asceticism, but by meditation and a resolute refusal either to injure the sense-organs or to be distracted by the allurements of sense-experience. Finally, the aspirant 'who has attained the highest Aryan Wisdom and has thus come to the end of the Way, knows the complete destruction of anguish'.[21] This is *Nirvāna*, which

> will not fail the man who has so tamed himself and developed himself that he is prepared physically, morally and mentally and in wisdom for the vision of it while he is deeply absorbed in meditation. Its unspeakable bliss cannot be described, it has to be experienced.

---

[18] *Ibid.*, pp. 280 f.   [19] *Ibid.*, p. 281.   [20] *Ibid.*, p. 283.   [21] *Ibid.*, p.288.

It is for the here and now rather than a kind of heaven
to be entered into by a virtuous man when he dies.
Perhaps it has therefore become less difficult to answer
the question that many people find perplexing: 'Who is
it that enjoys *Nirvāna* if there is not much left of the
man so-and-so after he has died?' The question framed
thus is inept and does not fit. Rather should it be
asked: Who enjoys *Nirvāna* here and now? The answer
is the adept in meditation. For *Nirvāna* may be seen
here in this very life.[22]

Then, when the Theravādin has 'done all there was to be
done to shed off the burden of "self" and cut off the binding
fetters', no fuel for a further rebirth remains in him, 'he no
longer grasps after anything in the "world", and while he still
lives here, his *karma* becomes exhausted. . . .' So he attains
parinirvāna. He will go on living on earth until his body
dies, after which he is 'free from all becomings'.[23]

The Theravādin thus has no strictly *theological* problem
about why the universe is as it is, or why sentient beings have
the cravings for existence and 'becoming' which cause such
deep anguish – or, for that matter, why he has to face temptation in the form of that 'inner enemy' who is personified as
Māra, a kind of Buddhist Satan. His 'Gospel' is, indeed, one
of the *possibility* of deliverance; but it entails a hard
struggle, usually over aeons of time; it must be by his own
unaided efforts to follow the Teaching; and it may well be
thought that it involves a process of almost complete dehumanization.

When we turn to the Mahāyāna form of Buddhism the
major difference is that man is no longer left to follow the
Teaching without any outside help. The Dharma itself is
basically the same, with the four Aryan Truths and the
Aryan Eightfold Path. But Conze remarks on a new

[22] *Ibid.*, pp. 289 f. One can see, here, one of the roots of Zen-Buddhism.
[23] *Ibid.*, pp. 291 f.

emphasis on 'loving kindness and compassion, subordinate virtues in the older Buddhism', which now 'move right into the centre of the picture'; on 'compassionate beings, called "Bodhisattvas",[24] whose main claim to our gratitude lies in that they sacrifice their lives for the welfare of all'; and on the fact that there is a new eschatological interest shown in a fervent hope of a 'second coming of the Buddha, as Maitreya'. These are intriguing developments when we realize that 'the literature which sets out the specific Mahāyāna doctrines is attested only for the beginning of the Christian era'; that occasionally 'we find close verbal co-incidences between the Christian and the Mahāyāna Scriptures'; and that it was 'in the two regions of India which were in contact with the Mediterranean' (South India, and North-West India) that the Mahāyāna 'seems to have originated'.[25]

But the two outstanding contributions of the Mahāyāna to Buddhist thought are 'the creation of the Bodhisattva ideal and the elaboration of the doctrine of "Emptiness".' A Bodhisattva (which literally means a 'being' or 'essence' of enlightenment) is a person who, in his essential being, yearns to attain full enlightenment, and thus become a Buddha; but he selflessly postpones his entrance into *Nirvāṇa* in order to help suffering creatures in this *saṃsāric* world. He is 'said to be dominated by two forces – compassion and wisdom. Compassion governs his conduct towards his fellow beings, wisdom his attitude to Reality'. It was, indeed, its teaching about Bodhisattvas which enabled the Mahāyāna to spread all over Central and South-East Asia, for their compassion for others, naturally enough, made a strong appeal to struggling humanity. Many stories

---

[24] The Theravādins only acknowledge one Bodhisattva – the one who, in the form of Gautama, went on to Buddhahood.   [25] Cf. Edward Conze, 'Buddhism: the Mahāyāna', in *The Concise Encyclopedia of Living Faiths*, pp. 293 f.

are told of Bodhisattvas who were willing to sacrifice their own lives even for animals; for the Buddhist believes not only that 'all beings are alike in that they dislike suffering, but they are also all capable of enlightenment. Each of them is a potential Buddha'.[26]

Yet this compassion must, in a Bodhisattva, always go hand in hand with wisdom. And this inevitably represents a potential point of tension. It is not only that he may be torn between his selfless desire to make others happy and his other-worldly goal of attaining Enlightenment, but also that it is far from obvious how he can in fact help others best. The problem can be put in a way which, *mutatis mutandis*, the Christian can easily enough understand:

> The highest good is said to be the gift of the Dharma. In that case the gift of anything else, in so far as it increases people's worldly welfare, may militate against the development of their spiritual potentialities, for it may bind them still further to this world and increase their worries and anxieties. Should we then wish to increase the material welfare of the people, or should we not?[27]

There is a good deal of discussion about this and kindred subjects, it seems, in Mahāyāna texts. It is obvious, for example, that the provision of adequate social services leaves much to be desired in most of the countries in which Buddhism flourishes; and it is equally clear that this is too widespread and radical a problem to be solved by private benevolence and charity. Any significant rise in the standard of living must, in reality, depend on the introduction of modern technology and schemes designed to enhance the productivity of labour. But this, in its turn, gives rise to a further problem. On the one hand the 'compassion' which the Mahāyāna emphasizes should make

[26] *Ibid.*, pp. 297 f.   [27] *Ibid.*, pp. 299.

Mahāyānists only too pleased to contemplate any prospect of eliminating extreme poverty, of providing better facilities for the sick and suffering, and of establishing a more efficient and humane administration of justice. On the other hand the 'wisdom' they extol teaches them that all these benefits can be obtained only by the acceptance of a new and technological organization of society which is far from conducive to spiritual life as they know it. To the mind of a Bodhisattva, moreover, this dilemma must be especially acute. He is firmly set on the path to a 'cognitive insight into a Reality which transcends this fleeting world, and all the beings in it'. Almost inevitably, one who has perceived this reality will long to withdraw into it. No more re-born, he will himself be immune to the fear of poverty, sickness or injustice. But he will also be lost to those whom he wants to help. Viewed from the angle of true reality, moreover, he will find it difficult to take their problems very seriously, for the whole of humanity 'will appear to him as a mass of nonentities constantly worrying over nothing in particular. This is a specially important point in Buddhism, which has always taught that persons are not really "persons", but only imagine that they are, whereas in strict fact they *are* nonentities'.[28]

In point of fact, Mahāyānists teach that enlightenment does not always entail the desire to help others. Among the enlightened some are unselfish, others much less so. Among the latter they number the Arhants of the Hīnayāna, while the unselfish types are Buddhas and Bodhisattvas. But this only becomes a *theological* problem when Mahāyānists, not content with regarding the Buddha as an infallible guide in spiritual matters, go on to claim, first, that he is omniscient, and knows everything; secondly, that this means that he *is* everything there is, and has become identical either with the

[28] Cf. *Ibid.*, p. 300.

Absolute, or with the sum total of existence; and, thirdly, that 'this Buddha — all knowing, all wise, all there is — is also all-compassionate'.[29] But, on this basis, what are we to think of the Buddha now that he has 'passed away' into the vast 'Emptiness' which is *Nirvāṇa*? And how can all the Buddhas — who, on this reasoning, would now seem to be virtually indistinguishable from each other — possess to perfection the apparently contradictory states of imperturbable even-mindedness, boundless compassion, and full emptiness? No wonder Edward Conze remarks that, from our lowly perspective, 'the transcendental world of self-extinction teems with apparent inconsistencies'.[30] By contrast, the Bodhisattvas remain in close contact with ordinary people because they experience the same passions as they do, although these passions do not have the same effect on Bodhisattvas nor produce the same pollution as in others. Unlike Buddhas, they have not 'become everything'; so we can still, in some measure, understand them, and we can appreciate that, while always intent on their transcendental goal, they still experience enough fellowship with us to feel:

> Can there be bliss when all that lives must suffer?
> Shalt thou be saved and hear the whole world cry?[31]

But the paradox of Mahāyāna Buddhism is that, while the gulf between even a Bodhisattva and a Buddha who is 'the sum total of everything there is' would seem to be almost infinite, yet

> only one single little obstacle separates him and us from Buddhahood, and that is the belief in a self, the belief that he is a separate individual, the inveterate tendency to indulge in what the texts call 'I-making and Mine-making'.[32]

In this last respect, then, there is only a very short step from

---

[29] *Ibid.*, p. 301.   [30] *Ibid.*, p. 301.   [31] H. P. Blavatasky, *The Voice of Silence*, p. 78 — Quoted by Edward Conze, *Ibid.*, p. 302.   [32] *Ibid.*, p. 302.

the Mahāyāna doctrine to that of the Advaita Vedānta school of Hindu thought, except that it is exceedingly difficult to regard an Absolute possessed of all-compassion as entirely impersonal. But, in spite of the teaching about 'only one single little obstacle' between us and Buddhahood, the Mahāyāna in practice distinguish ten stages through which a Bodhisattva must pass on his way to Buddhahood. With the sixth of these he has, by his understanding of Emptiness, come face to face with Reality itself and is entitled to *Nirvāṇa*; but this he renounces voluntarily. From now on he will never be re-born except supernaturally, and he acquires many qualities which raise him to the status of a celestial being and enable him, in some measure, to become a saviour of ordinary mortals. These Bodhisattvas are, therefore, as worthy of worship as the Buddhas, and some Mahāyānists apparently think that they are more so.[33] But the growing belief in mythical Bodhisattvas – such as Amitābha [34] (who subsequently became a Buddha) – was in point of fact preceded by the belief in mythical Buddhas, for this concept developed in the Mahāsanghika school of Hīnayāna Buddhism within a century of Gautama's death. It was in this group that the historical Buddha began to be thought of as a mere 'magical creation' of the transcendental Buddha, a 'fictitious creature sent by him to appear in the world and to teach its inhabitants'.[35] It is, indeed, in some such way as this, presumably, that Hindus often regard Gautama as an *avatār* of Vishnu. But the Mahāsanghikas – followed, in due course, by the Mahāyāna – greatly enhanced the importance of the transcendental Buddha to ordinary people, for they insisted that he has not, in reality, disappeared into *Nirāṇa* but, with infinite compassion, will conjure up, until the end of time, 'all kinds of forms which will help all kinds of beings in

[33] *Ibid.*, p. 305. [34] Cp. pp. 29 f. above. [35] Edward Conze, *op. cit.*, p. 307.

diverse ways'. Nor will his help be limited to those who are able to understand his more abstruse teachings, but as a Bodhisattva he will be re-born in the 'states of woe' — quite voluntarily, of course — even as an animal, a ghost, or one of the denizens of hell, so that he may be able to help people whose condition is such that his wisdom teaching would be incomprehensible to them. It must not be thought, moreover, that Buddhas are confined to this earth, for they fill the entire universe.[36]

It was around AD 300 that the Buddhology of the Mahā-yāna was finally formulated in the doctrine of the *Three Bodies*.[37] A Buddha exists on three levels: he has (1) a fictitious, conjured-up body, (2) an enjoyment body and (3) a Dharma body. The 'fictitious' or 'conjured-up' body is, of course, that of a historical Buddha during his time on earth — and in the fifteenth century this concept of 'fictitious bodies' took a form in Tibet which almost everyone has heard of but which very few understand. I refer, of course, to Dalai Lamas and 'Living Buddhas'. The point which is misunderstood is 'the essential difference between ordinary people and accomplished saints in their manner of coming into the world'. An ordinary person inherits the *karma* that he, or someone else, has accumulated in some previous exist-ence. But this does not apply to the celestial Bodhisattvas or Buddhas, who can at any time conjure up phantom bodies which are outwardly just like ordinary bodies. They use these as a kind of 'puppet' to help or to convert other people. But this phenomenon should not be regarded as in any sense an incarnation of the celestial being concerned, but rather as a 'free creation of his magical power'.[38] Such are the Lamas. A Buddha's 'enjoyment body', on the other hand, is a supernatural, radiant sort of body in which he 'appears to superhuman beings and to the celestial Bodhisattvas in

---

[36] Cf., *Ibid.*, p. 307.   [37] Cf. p. 31 above.   [38] Cf. *Ibid.*, p. 308.

unearthly realms which his merit has created'; whereas the 'Dharma-body' is, of course, the Buddha seen in the Absolute.

The growth of Lamaism in Tibet represents, in reality, an adaptation of Buddhist doctrine to the Bon religion which previously prevailed in that country. As such, it is an instance of the way in which Mahāyāna Buddhism was prepared to gloss over the differences between Buddhist and non-Buddhist doctrines and to absorb a great deal of any religion from which it made converts. As a consequence, we find in China and Japan examples of a syncretism in which it accommodated a number of Taoist, Shintō, Manichaean, shamanistic and other views. But inevitably, of course, this exposed Mahāyāna monks to the danger of lapsing into both a moral and doctrinal laxity.[39]

Dr Conze, however, emphasizes that this facility for adaptation, together with the strange beliefs which different sections of Mahāyāna Buddhism profess, all in fact represent part of the 'vast phantasmogoria' of a world of illusion. In actual reality, he says,

> there are no Buddhas, no Bodhisattvas, no perfections, no stages, and no paradises – none of all this. All these conceptions have no reference to anything that is actually there, and concern a world of mere phantasy. They are just expedients, concessions to the multitude of the ignorant, provisional constructions of thought, which become superfluous after having served their purpose. For the Mahāyāna is a 'vehicle', designed to ferry people across to salvation. When the goal of the Beyond has been reached, it can safely be discarded. . . . All multiplicity, all separation, all duality is a sign of falseness. Everything apart from the One,

---

[39] Cf. *ibid.*, p. 310.

also called 'Emptiness' or 'Suchness', is devoid of real existence, and whatever may be said about it is ultimately untrue, false and nugatory, though perhaps permissible if the salvation of beings requires it. The ability to frame salutary statements and to act in conformity with people's needs, springs from a faculty called 'skill in means', which comes to a Bodhisattva only . . . after the 'perfection of wisdom' has thoroughly shown him the emptiness of everything.[40]

But what is this 'Emptiness' to which Buddhists so often refer? It has been described as transcendental reality 'beyond the grasp of intellectual comprehension and verbal expression', and is also called 'Suchness' and the 'One'. It is 'Suchness', we are told, 'if and when one takes it "such as it is", without adding anything to it or subtracting anything from it'. And it is the 'One' because it alone is real, and the multiple world is merely a product of our imagination. But if all is in fact the same, then it follows that, in the ultimate analysis, the Absolute is identical with the relative, the Unconditioned is the same as the conditioned, and *Nirvāna* does not really differ from *samsāra*.[41] This would certainly explain why the Bodhisattvas are said not to leave or abandon the *samsāric* world,[42] were we not also told that there are in reality no such beings as Bodhisattvas!

It seems clear, then, that the Mahāyāna's answer to the problem of suffering and evil is not, basically, very different from that of Theravāda Buddhism. The latter, as we have seen, teaches that sentient beings, by their very nature, crave to exist, to become and even to possess; and that this craving inevitably leads to suffering. The only cure for this suffering is to extirpate all such craving by a strictly disciplined life (which may well extend over many different existences, in the course of which the *karma* a man has

[40] *Ibid.*, p. 309.   [41] Cf. *Ibid.*, p. 312.   [42] Cf. pp. 145 f., 148 f. above.

inherited may finally work itself out) and by learning the secret of deep meditation which will at length lead to a state of peace in which sensory experiences cease to disturb and all desire is at last silenced. The Mahāyāna, which in reality starts from much the same postulates, certainly gives the appearance of having abandoned the arid atheism of the orthodox Theravāda, and its emphatic repudiation of any external or supernatural help in this stern struggle, in favour of a quasi-theism which sometimes takes a polytheistic, sometimes a pantheistic, but most basically of all — it seems — a monistic form. As such it offers its devotees supernatural help from compassionate Bodhisattvas and benevolent Buddhas in this vital quest to eliminate the phantom of 'self' either in the course of this life or in some more congenial realm to which the Bodhisattva will obtain his devotees' entrance. As a consequence, a blind faith in the chosen Bodhisattva takes the place — to some measure at least — of the stern effort to work out one's own salvation. Yet it seems that a strong case can be made out for suggesting that all this is illusory, a 'skill in means', a way of pandering to the needs of the ignorant or gullible. But, leaving that point aside, a Christian is bound to ask himself, I think, whether the quest itself is right. He is certainly encouraged in his own faith to 'deny himself', to 'put to death . . . whatever belongs to [our] earthly nature: sexual immorality, impurity, lust, evil desires and greed',[43] and to 'take up [his] cross' and follow Christ. But this is *not* intended to lead to any process of 'dehumanization', for he is equally commanded to 'clothe [himself] with compassion, kindness, humility, gentleness and patience'; to live a life of loving fellowship with others; and to do all that he does, whether in word or deed, 'in the name of the Lord Jesus, giving thanks to God the Father through him'.[44] He is also told that he has been 'given all

[43] Colossians 3:5.   [44] Colossians 3:12-17.

things richly to enjoy'[45] and that he should 'rejoice in the Lord always'.[46]

The aim of the Buddhist is to eliminate suffering and reach a status from which he can look back at all ordinary human life as something less than wholly real. So it is useless, as I see it, to ask him *why* sentient beings are born with these insistent cravings which must, of necessity, engender so much suffering and pain. To this, as an atheist or even a theistic pantheist or a monist, he has no sort of answer. This is how things are, and that is all there is to it. Now it is perfectly true that the Christian, too, can make no claim – as we shall see – to understand the basic mystery of suffering and evil. But he does have at least a partial explanation of the reasons behind *some* suffering. What is more, he believes that even the suffering that he cannot understand may be transmuted into gain on at least three levels. First, he can himself learn many lessons from it – a subject to which we shall return. Secondly, God can and does comfort him in it with a comfort that he can subsequently share with others.[47] Thirdly, he can in some sense participate in the sufferings of the Christ he seeks to follow.[48] And that brings me to the basic point of all, which I will express in Bishop Stephen Neill's words:

> Why suffer? That is the ultimate question. It comes to sharp and challenging expression in the contrast between the serene and passionless Buddha and the tortured figure on the Cross. In Jesus we see One who looked at suffering with eyes as clear and calm as those of the Buddha. He saw no reason to reject it, to refuse it, to eliminate it. He took it into himself and felt the fullness of its bitterness and horror; by the grace of God he tasted death for every man. Others suffer; he will

[45] 1 Timothy 6:17.   [46] Philippians 4:4.   [47] Cf. 2 Corinthians 1:4.
[48] Philippians 3:10.

suffer with them and for them, and will go on suffering
till the end of time. But he does not believe that suffering is wholly evil; by the power of God it can be transformed into a redemptive miracle. Suffering is not an
obstacle to deliverance; it can become part of the
deliverance itself. And what he was he bids his children
be — the world's sufferers, in order that through suffering the world may be brought back to God. The
Buddhist ideal is that of passionless benevolence. The
Christian ideal is that of compassion. When argument
has done its best, we must perhaps leave the two ideals
face to face. We can only ask our Buddhist friend to
look long and earnestly on the Cross of Christ, and to
ask himself whether, beyond the peace of the Buddha,
there may not be another dimension of peace to the
attainment of which there is no way other than the
Way of the Cross.[49]

The fact that both Judaism and Islam believe firmly in
one true God who is both 'personal' and Lord of all makes it
a matter of particular interest to see how they view the problem of suffering and evil. How was it that the Jews, who from
the time of Abraham, as we have seen,[50] have regarded
themselves as God's covenant people, have interpreted the
unique sufferings that they have had to undergo down the
centuries? It is immediately clear, from the Old Testament
itself, that they have frequently accepted defeat, calamity
and exile as a just punishment for their national sin and
apostasy — sometimes as coming from the hand of a justly
angry God, and sometimes from a grieved but loving Father.
They have learnt by experience, too, that sometimes their
God would not only forgive their shortcomings but even
'restore the years that the locusts had eaten',[51] while at other

---

[49] *Christian Faith and Other Faiths* (OUP, London, 1961), pp. 123 f.
[50] Cf. pp. 44 f., 52 f. above.   [51] Joel 2:25.

times an individual's heartfelt repentance would result in the forgiveness of his sin and the immediate restoration of his fellowship with God, but not in the remission of some temporal punishment or the removal of the entail of what he had done.[52]

But there are also many passages in the Old Testament that testify to the fact that suffering was not always, by any means, regarded as a punishment for sin, but as a process of trial, testing and sifting, the acceptance of which in an obedient and filial spirit would result in a greater maturity of character and a more intimate knowledge of God and his love. Such, pre-eminently, was the supreme testing of Abraham recorded in Genesis 22; and it was the way in which he responded to this test that prompted the divine promise:

> I swear by myself, declares the Lord, that because you have done this and have not withheld your son, your only son, I will surely bless you and make your descendents as numerous as the stars in the sky and as the sands on the sea shore. Your descendants will take possession of the cities of their enemies, and through your offspring all nations on earth will be blessed, because you have obeyed me.[53]

Again, the book of Job seems to be a sublime and divinely-inspired drama devoted to this very subject. As E. S. P. Heavenor justly states:

> It is a striking reminder of the inadequacy of human horizons for a proper understanding of the problem of suffering. All the human figures in the drama speak in total ignorance of Satan's allegations against Job's piety, reported in the prologue, and of the resultant divine permission to prove his point, if he can. Against

[52] Cf. David's sin in regard to Bathsheba and Uriah.   [53] Genesis 22:16 ff.

the background of the prologue Job's sufferings appear, not as damning evidence of the divine judgement upon him, as his friends had sought to establish, but as proof of the divine confidence in him. We must avoid the *naiveté* of using language which might seem to indicate that an omniscient God needed such a demonstration of his servant's integrity, to silence, as it were, some tiny doubt in His mind: but we are entitled to find here a suggestion of the truth that now we can only 'see in a mirror dimly'. Job and the others were trying to fit together the pieces of a puzzle without having all the pieces within their grasp. Consequently the book of Job is an eloquent commentary on the inadequacy of the human mind to reduce the complexity of suffering to some consistent pattern.[54]

In other words, the twin principles that he 'who sows wickedness reaps trouble',[55] and that 'the Lord disciplines those he loves',[56] were both fully recognized by the Jews, as was also the fact that a loving God 'does not treat us as our sins deserve or repay us according to our iniquities'.[57]

There can, moreover, be no doubt that the Jews came to regard the sufferings of the righteous as having an expiatory or atoning significance. This thought runs through Isaiah 40-53; and G. R. Driver states that the words of Isaiah 53:11 'were echoed down the ages, being applied in each successive generation to some just man or Messianic figure who suffered an unjust fate'.[58] The Community Rule of Qumran, again, provides that the twelve laymen and three priests of the Community Council should 'expiate iniquity through

---

[54] Article on 'Job' in *The New Bible Commentary Revised* (ed. by D. Guthrie, J. A. Motyer, A. M. Stibbs and D. J. Wiseman, Inter-Varsity Press, London, 1970), p. 422.   [55] Proverbs 22:8.   [56] Proverbs 3:12.
[57] Psalm 103:10.   [58] *The Judaean Scrolls* (Blackwell, Oxford, 1965), p. 257.

deeds of justice and the anguish of the refining furnace'.[59] At a later date, moreover, Yehuda Halevi placed the mystery of Israel, as a 'mystical community whose election and suffering are mysteriously and inextricably interwoven', in the centre of his theodicy.[60] It is clear, however, that quotations from Isaiah 53 are rare in Rabbinic literature, and Mr H. Loewe explicitly states that 'Because of the christological interpretation given to the chapter by Christians, it is omitted from the series of prophetical lessons (*Haftarot*) for the Deuteronomy Sabbaths', and adds that this omission 'is deliberate and striking'.[61] But none of this really touches the *origin* of moral evil as such, which was attributed by the Jews to the deliberate disobedience of our first parents instigated by a tempter who can be understood only in terms of an early cosmic 'Fall' before recorded history began.

The problem of national suffering and humiliation scarcely arose in Islam in the early years of the Hijra which, for the Arabs, represented an almost unbroken success story. The experience of individual suffering must, however, have been as common in Muslim countries as in the rest of the contemporary world. But resignation and fortitude have always been salient Muslim virtues, for Muslims have, for the most part, lived up to the name by which they call themselves: those who 'submit' to God and whatever he, in his utter sovereignty, sees fit to do. He is their Lord (*Rabb*), and they are his servants or slaves (*'abīd*); so it is not for them to question, or complain about, his sovereign will. This attitude has, of course, all too often in the past resulted in

[59] *Ibid.*, p. 579. Cf. G. Vermes, *The Dead Sea Scrolls* (Collins, London, 1977), p. 91; Matthew Black, 'The Dead Sea Scrolls and Christian Origins', in *The Scrolls and Christianity* (SPCK, London, 1969), p. 101; and A. R. C. Leaney, *The Rule of Qumran and its Meaning* (SCM Press, London, 1966), p. 213.   [60] *Selected Poems of Jehudah Halevi* (tr. Nina Salaman, Philadelphia, 1946), quoted by Zwi Werblowsky, *op. cit.*, p. 25.   [61] Cf. C. G. Montefiori and H. Loewe, *Rabbinic Anthology* (Macmillan, London, 1938), p. 544.

an almost blind fatalism which has stultified initiative and impeded progress; but this sort of fatalism is rapidly disappearing today in the more enlightened parts of the Muslim world. The fact remains, however, that to the pious Muslim everything that happens is not merely an outworking of the purposes of God but occurs by his direct fiat;[62] and while it is a comparatively venial fault to fail to obey the divine Law in some particular respect, it is rank apostasy to doubt its validity or call it in question. The average Muslim, moreover, is – as we have seen – much more concerned with God's Law than with his Love, which he commonly thinks of chiefly as his 'mercy'; and it is, perhaps, relevant in this context that Muslims habitually refer to someone who has died as 'the one to whom mercy has been shown'. But, however this may be, orthodox Islam certainly believes that both good and ill, calamity and prosperity, come directly from the hand of God. It is true that the Mu'tazila held that God commands the good because it is intrinsically good and forbids the evil because it is inherently evil – or, in other words, that he habitually cares for the welfare of his creatures; but the orthodox Ash'ariyya would have none of this, and insisted that virtue and vice depended solely on the divine decree.[63] Even the Mu'tazila, moreover, were content to state their doctrinal conviction in general terms, and did not venture to examine its validity in detail.

It often seems to be in Christendom that people find it hardest to accept the sufferings and calamities of life without blaming God. This is partly, of course, because even nominal Christians are apt to think, at such times, in terms of a personal God who, they know, is alleged to be both all-loving and all-powerful – and there are plenty of situations in which they find an almost irresistible impulse to ask 'Why, then, did he allow *that* to happen?' They cannot, like

[62] Cf. pp. 94, 100 f., 119 above.   [63] Cf. p. 88 above.

the Hindu, attribute the calamities that fall suddenly on some hapless individual or community (either from the vagaries of Nature or the cruelties of man) to the outworking of the entail of *karma* from lives lived long ago. Nor can they, like the Buddhist, regard suffering as the inevitable concomitant of all sentient existence, against which the sole protection is to try to eliminate every feeling or desire so radically that they would virtually cease to be human. Again, neither their knowledge nor acceptance of monistic philosophy is such as to enable them to dismiss all phenomenal existence as, in the final analysis, no more than a passing illusion in the light of the one and only Absolute Reality which underlies all things. And they find it desperately difficult to say 'Kismet' and leave it there, as the Turk or Arab is alleged to do. Yet the nominal Christian would take it very much amiss if God were continually to intervene in his own life to stop him doing anything that might injure the feelings or damage the interests of somone else; and he finds it a baffling problem to realize that suffering comes from many different sources and causes, and may therefore find at least a partial explanation in a variety of different ways.

Even the convinced Christian, moreover, frequently finds it very hard to accept suffering in the right spirit. Often enough it is in fact the result of our own disobedience to God's laws, and we must learn again 'that word of *encouragement*' that addresses us as sons:

> My son, do not make light of the Lord's discipline,
>   and do not lose heart when he rebukes you,
> because the Lord disciplines those he *loves*,
>   and he punishes everyone he accepts as a son.

We need to remember, moreover, that

> we have all had human fathers who disciplined us and
> we respected them for it. How much more should we

submit to the Father of our spirits and live! Our fathers disciplined us for a little while as they thought best; but God disciplines us for our good, that we may share in his holiness. No discipline seems pleasant at the time, but painful. Later on, however, it produces a harvest of righteousness and peace for those who have been trained by it.[64]

Again, suffering as a result of our own sin or folly may often be explained not so much as a special act of personal chastisement as the normal outworking of the eternal law: 'Do not be deceived: God is not mocked. A man reaps what he sows'[65] – a law which, as we have seen, is common to both Eastern and Hebrew thought.

At other times, moreover, our suffering may have nothing whatever to do with our own sin, but may result from the malice or carelessness of others – permitted by God, so far as we are concerned, so that he may 'work' in it for our ultimate good in a growing conformity 'to the likeness of his Son'.[66] After all, we are told that even Jesus himself was 'made perfect through suffering'[67] and 'learnt obedience in the school of suffering'[68]; and if he needed to learn in such a hard school in order to attain human perfection, then how much more must we? Only so, we are told, could he become a High Priest who could 'sympathize with our weaknesses', because he has himself been tempted and tested 'in every way, just as we are'.[69] This is why we can always 'approach the throne of grace with confidence, so that we may receive mercy and find grace to help us in our time of need[70] – and, indeed, may be in a position to 'comfort those in any trouble with the comfort we ourselves have received from God'.[71]

But what can we say about the heart-rending calamities

[64] Hebrews 12:5 ff., part of which is a quotation from Proverbs 3: 11 f., (my italics).   [65] Galatians 6:7.   [66] Romans 8:28, 29.
[67] Hebrews 2:10.   [68] Hebrews 5:8.   [69] Hebrews 4:15.
[70] Hebrews 4:16.   [71] 2 Corinthians 2:4.

and hardships which fall on some individuals and communities? This represents one of the most difficult problems we ever have to face; and we need to remember that Jesus himself, although he spoke often enough about suffering, never — so far as we know — really *explained* it. We cannot, I repeat, believe that it represents the *karma* that the people concerned inherit from some supposed previous existence; but I think we can — and must — see it as in some sense the entail of human sin in general — and, behind that, of some cosmic 'Fall' that we do not really understand. What seems clear is that God created man as a rational and moral being who has, within limits, the freedom to choose; that man made the wrong moral choice and became involved in this cosmic sin; and that God's fair creation is now sadly out of tune. But if God is omniscient he must have known that this would happen; so why did he embark on this course? The answer, I presume, is that one of his basic purposes was that he might ultimately bring 'many sons to glory'[72] — that is, to the glory of being sons of God, in the full sense of that term, for some end which we can now only dimly and partially perceive; and no mere robot, but only a rational and moral creature, could ever become a son of God. But, if this is the answer, it must mean that the glory of what God has in view will, in the end, make all the suffering, frustration and pain that has been experienced throughout the history of the world worthwhile. I do not see how else we can understand St Paul's words:

> I consider that our present sufferings are not worth comparing with the glory that will be revealed in us. The creation waits in eager expectation for the sons of God to be revealed. For the creation was subjected to frustration, not by its own choice, but by the will of the one who subjected it, in hope that the creation itself will

[72] Hebrews 2:10.

be liberated from its bondage to decay and brought into the glorious freedom of the children of God.[73]

In the meantime it is, of course, an inexplicable mystery how this entail of evil and suffering operates and is apportioned;[74] but we can at least see that for God always to avert the calamities which befall both individuals and communities would involve such continual acts of supernatural intervention as would completely change the very nature and structure of the world in which we live.

Nor should we, of course, forget that pain often serves a most useful and beneficial function – that of alerting our attention to, and giving due warning of, something which, if ignored or persisted in, would cause far more suffering. The scalding that instinctively prevents even a small child from putting its fingers into a fire, or playing with piping hot water, is an obvious case in point – as is also the pain in some part of our body which induces us to visit a doctor before an unsuspected disease reaches dangerous proportions. And the same principle obtains in regard to the judgements of God. It is not for nothing, for example, that in the last book in the Bible the seven Trumpets of warning[75] precede both the seven Plagues[76] and the seven Bowls of God's Wrath.[77] On a more personal level, moreover, it is a matter of common experience that, when everything in life seems to go well, we all too easily become immersed in things that are temporal; and we need some disturbing factor, at the very least, to turn our eyes to those things that our eternal. If I remember C. S. Lewis's words aright, he once wrote that if God whispers to us in life's pleasures, he positively shouts at us in our pains; and it was certainly he who wrote:

> No doubt Pain as God's megaphone is a terrible instrument; it may lead to final and unrepented rebellion.

---

[73] Romans 8:18-21.   [74] Cf. Luke 13:1-6; John 9:3; etc.
[75] Revelation chapters 8-11.   [76] Revelation chapter 15.
[77] Revelation chapter 16.

> But it gives the only opportunity the bad man can have
> for amendment. It removes the veil; it plants the flag of
> truth within the fortress of a rebel soul.[78]

But here I must, I think, demur. Even with the rebellious
I believe that it is often some experience of God's love,
goodness, or sheer 'grace' that moves men to repentance.
But if this fails to move us, then surely pain, calamity,
bereavement or any other suffering is, in the circumstances,
itself a manifestation of his love and grace. The worst fate
we can ever experience is for God to 'leave us alone', or 'give
us up'.[79] It all depends, in the final analysis, on which is the
more important: ease in this life, or eternal salvation. But
let me hasten to add that no such consideration can justify
the activities of, say, the 'Holy Inquisition'. It is God alone
who knows the human heart and can wean it from unbelief
or rebellion to himself; and for man to attempt to effect
such a transformation by force is not only wrong but almost
always counter-productive. Nor do I believe that the New
Testament in reality supports what Professor Hick terms the
traditional doctrine of hell: 'eternal suffering inflicted by
God upon those of His creatures who have sinfully rejected
Him'.[80] St Paul, for example, refers to those who 'will be
punished with everlasting *destruction*',[81] and the last book in
the Bible speaks of the 'second death'[82] — both of which
terms seem to envisage a judgement which is final in its
effect rather than eternal in conscious suffering — while the
words in Mark 9:48 'where their worm does not die, and the
fire is not quenched' are clearly a quotation from Isaiah
66:24 (where they cannot have been meant literally), and the
very term Gehenna is a reference to the valley of the sons of
Hinnon, which was the place where the rubbish of Jerusalem
was burnt up or was consumed by maggots. It is in this

[78] *The Problem of Pain* (Collins, Fontana Library, 1957), p. 83.
[79] Romans 1:24, 26, 28.   [80] *Evil and the God of Love*, p. 377. Cf. footnote 91 below.   [81] 2 Thessalonians 2:9.   [82] Revelation 20:6.

context that J. S. Whale wrote:

> I know that it is no longer fashionable to talk about
> Hell, one good reason for this being that to make
> religion into a prudential insurance policy is to degrade
> it. The Faith is not a Fire-escape. But in rejecting the
> old mythology of eternity as grotesque and even im-
> moral, many people make the mistake of rejecting the
> truth it illustrated (which is rather like rejecting a book
> as untrue because the pictures in it are bad). It is
> illogical to tell men that they must do the will of God
> and accept his gospel of grace if you also tell them that
> the obligation has no eternal significance. . . .[83]

But a further – and, essentially, a deeper – question lies
behind this whole problem: does God himself suffer in, and
with, suffering humanity? This thought would, I think, be
utterly repudiated by Advaita Vedānta Hindus, since it is inconceivable to them that the Absolute Reality could in any
sense suffer. Equally, it would be denied by Hindus of the
Sāṁkhya-Yoga school and by Theravādin Buddhists,
because neither the one nor the other believes in God, or
even in a 'Supreme Soul', while for Buddhists of the Mahāyāna persuasion any Buddha or Bodhisattva is beyond the
reach of suffering. Muslims, on the other hand, believe in
one God who is fully 'personal'; but they would reject with
horror the suggestion that he could in any way be affected
by his creatures. The God of Islam – as depicted by Muslim
theologians[84] rather than the Qur'ān – is much too transcendent for that. But so, too, is the God of much Rabbinic and
Patristic thought, for Jewish and Christian theologians were,
far too often, obsessed by the Hellenistic concept of an unmoved, unchanging, philosophical abstraction of perfection
rather than thinking in terms of the living God of the Bible.
That God is, indeed, 'immutable' in his character, and

[83] *Christian Doctrine* (CUP, 1950), pp. 186 f.   [84] Cf. pp. 100 f. above.

always faithful to his promises, is certainly true; but this does not mean that he does not take new initiatives – as in the Creation, the Incarnation, the Atonement, the New Covenant, and much else. The Old Testament, too, depicts Yahweh as being 'distressed' or 'afflicted' in all the afflictions of his people,[85] and as grieving over unfaithful Israel in the way that a loving and forgiving husband grieves over an unfaithful wife.[86] In Christian teaching, moreover, the thought of God suffering because of the sins, follies and sorrows of his creatures has often been confined to the incarnate Son, or even to Jesus exclusively in his *human* nature. But I am myself convinced that this is due to the influence of Greek philosophy rather than biblical teaching. It no doubt made sense to Cyril to affirm that 'the impassible Logos suffered in the passible flesh', or that the incarnate Lord 'suffered impassibly'; but for us today it was Jesus himself, God-in-manhood, who wept over Jerusalem and 'bore our sins in his body on the tree',[87] for it was the whole person who underwent these experiences. Nor could Paul even have asserted, in any meaningful way, that 'God demonstrates his own love for us in this: While we were still sinners, Christ died for us'[88] unless he had believed that there was an essential unity between Father and Son.

In point of fact the term 'impassibility', as the late Professor Oliver Quick insisted, can be used in three different senses:

> *External* passibility refers to the relation of one being to another, or the capacity to be acted on from outside oneself. *Internal* passibility, on the other hand, refers to those fluctuating emotions and moods which a man experiences within himself. And *sensational* passibility

---

[85] Cf. Isaiah 63:9.   [86] Cf. Hosea, *passim*. In this context cf. also J. Skinner on Jeremiah 45:4 f., in *Prophecy and Religion* (CUP, 1922), pp. 347 f.   [87] 1 Peter 2:24.   [88] Romans 5:8.

denotes the capacity to experience pleasure and pain, joy and sorrow.[89]

If we adopt this classification, then we must, I think, affirm that passibility in the second sense — fluctuating emotions and moods — cannot be postulated of God, who, as the Thirty-Nine Articles put it, is 'without body, parts or passions'; but it was integral to the experience of the incarnate Lord, who had a human soul as well as a human body. In both the first and third meanings of passibility, moreover, it is no doubt true that God is impassible in the sense that he is not subject to external constraint; but Professor Mascall has pointed out that Père Galot makes

> a fundamental distinction between the necessary order of God's being and the free order of his will. Immutability and impassibility belong to the former, but creation and redemption to the latter, in which love and suffering are really and not just verbally implicated. 'In God suffering belongs not to the order of necessity and of essence but to that of free initiative'. This involves no imperfection in God; just the opposite. 'He is sovereign, and sovereignty consists in acting in the freest manner, and in *not* being imprisoned in an inaccessible attitude'.[90]

None of this, again, makes any basic attempt to discuss the dilemma which is inherent in the origin of moral evil. As we have seen, this does not pose any acute problem for a polytheist or a dualist — or even, in a theological sense, for a

---

[89] This quotation comes from some as yet unpublished lectures given in Oxford University, for the loan of which I am indebted to Professor Donald MacKinnon.   [90] *Theology and the Gospel of Christ* (SPCK, London, 1977), pp. 182 f. The quotation from Galot is taken from *Vers une nouvelle christologie* (Gembloux, Duculot and Paris, Lethielleux, 1971), p. 172. This whole paragraph is substantially a quotation from my recent book *The Mystery of the Incarnation* (Hodder and Stoughton, London, 1978), pp. 151 f.

pantheist or a monist. But there is an obvious anomaly for the Christian in the very thought of moral evil being created by a holy and loving God.[91] I am myself content to postulate, however, that he did not create moral evil as such, but men and women with a certain freedom of moral choice; for only so could he bring 'many sons to glory'. But it is clear that this must have involved creating a world in which there was the *possibility* that they would make wrong moral choices, knowing (in his divine omniscience) that this is what they — and also, it seems, certain angelic beings — would in fact do, with all the suffering and misery that would follow. Yet he did it. And from this stark fact we can, I believe, draw two conclusions. First, that the final glory that he had in view would not only outweigh the intervening wretchedness, but even swallow it up; and, secondly, that there was no other way in which his purposes could be fulfilled. Even before the creation, moreover, he had planned the way of redemption — at a cost that we cannot begin to compute, not only to the Son who came, lived and died but also to the Father who 'sent' him. All down the centuries, too, he has himself suffered with and for his creatures. Our God is not an impersonal Absolute, a Supreme Soul, a First

[91] For a comprehensive discussion of the Christian approach to theodicy (a term defined in *Collins English Dictionary* as meaning both 'the branch of theology concerned with the attributes of God against objections resulting from physical and moral evil' and also 'the philosophical study of God and the destiny of the soul') cf. John Hick, *Evil and the God of Love* (Macmillan, London, 1966 — republished by Collins, London, in 1968 in the Fontana Library). This represents an admirable summary of the views of many different writers over the centuries, whom he classifies as basically following either the 'Augustinian' or the 'Irenaean' approach. Then, in a final section entitled 'A Theodicity for Today', Professor Hick gives a somewhat naive summary of what he terms 'the official Christian myth' regarding 'creation-fall-redemption' (which he describes as 'open to insuperable scientific, moral and logical objections') and the conclusions about this — and also about life beyond the grave — to which he had himself come.

Cause or a remote Creator. He is certainly transcendent, but he is also immanent in his creation and sensitive to all its sorrows and sins. And he demonstrated this supremely in the Incarnation, in which the eternal Son was willing to share our humanity; to be tempted in every way, just as we are';[92] to suffer an agonizing death; and even to experience, vicariously, the horror of that spiritual desolation which is the inevitable result of human sin. In this context I cannot forbear from quoting the last verse, only, of a poem I have quoted more fully elsewhere:[93]

> The other gods were strong; but Thou wast weak;
> They rode, but Thou didst stumble to a throne;
> But to our wounds only God's wounds can speak,
> And not a god has wounds, but Thou alone.[94]

---

[92] Hebrews 4:15.   [93] Cf. *The Mystery of the Incarnation*, p. 157.
[94] Edward Shillito, *Jesus of the Scars and Other Poems* – quoted by William Temple, *Readings in St John's Gospel* (Macmillan, London, 1942), p. 385.

EPILOGUE

The Law of God and
The Gospel

Up to now this book has stuck strictly to its title — The Law
of God and the Love of God — in the light of the teaching
and practice of what I hope is a reasonably representative
number of the world's religions. In this final chapter,
however, I want to change the emphasis from law and love
to law and the gospel. This may well seem to some who have
read the preceding chapters to be a matter of mere seman-
tics, or little more than playing with words. But this would
be a fundamental mistake. For whereas, at the human level,
the difference between law and love may, on occasion, be so
sharp as to amount to a contradiction,[1] there can be no basic
contradiction between God's law and his love, since his law
must of necessity be one manifestation — or, from another
point of view, sometimes the obverse side — of the love which
constitutes his very nature. Yet, although the gospel
represents the supreme embodiment of that love, there is a
real sense in which God's law and his gospel stand in stark
antithesis, as well as in vital relationship, to each other. So it
is the purpose of this final chapter to explore the difference,
as well as define the relationship, between God's law and the
gospel.

[1] But cf. Harold J. Berman, *The Interaction of Law and Religion*
(Abingdon Press, New York, 1974), especially pp. 81-91.

First, then, the antithesis between them, on which the Reformers put so great an emphasis. In their view all Scripture could, and should, be divided into 'two chief themes': Law and Gospel. To maintain the proper distinction between the one and the other was a matter of the utmost importance but extreme difficulty; and Luther himself said that 'anyone who knows how to distinguish the Gospel from the law should thank God and realize that he is a true theologian. In the time of temptation, I do not myself know how to do this as I ought.'[2] There is, however, probably as much loose thinking about the essential meaning of 'the Gospel' today as there was at the time of the Reformation, although the nature of the misunderstanding may, to some extent, have changed. In the sixteenth century the fundamental confusion arose from the concept that salvation could – and, indeed, should – be earned by a combination of piety and morality, to say nothing of indulgences, priestly absolutions and works of supererogation; and this misconception of the basis of acceptance with God is with us still, for the idea that we must somehow *earn* our forgiveness seems to represent a universal human instinct. But today this error is compounded by the fact that the word 'gospel' is often used as virtually synonymous with Christianity as such.

In a broad sense of the term this is, of course, understandable enough, for the English word 'gospel' represents the Anglo-Saxon *godspell* (or 'God's story') and is used to translate *euangelion,* a word which in classical Greek meant the reward given for good tidings, but in the New Testament and early Christian literature came to signify the good tidings themselves – or, to quote Professor F. F. Bruce, 'the good news that God in Jesus Christ has fulfilled his promises to Israel and that a way of salvation has been opened to

[2] Cf. Weimar Edition, Vol. 40, Pt. 1., p. 207 – on Galatians 2:14 in the commentary of 1531 (rev. 1535). Cf. also *A Dictionary of Christian Ethics* (ed. John Macquarrie, SCM Press, London, 1967), p. 193.

all'.[3] When, however, Paul said that the gospel had been 'revealed' and 'entrusted' to him by direct revelation from Christ himself,[4] and that even an angel from heaven who preached 'a different gospel — which is no gospel at all' — deserved to be 'eternally condemned',[5] he clearly gave it a much more precise meaning. And this more precise meaning is, I think, summed up in 1 Corinthians 15:1-8: namely, that 'Christ died for our sins according to the Scriptures, that he was buried, that he was raised on the third day according to the Scriptures, and that he appeared' after that to many of his disciples.[6] It was of this gospel that Paul was 'not ashamed, because it is the power of God for the salvation of everyone who believes: first for the Jew, then for the Gentile. For in the gospel a righteousness from God (or, as the RSV has it, 'God's way of righting wrong') is revealed, a righteousness which is by faith from first to last[7] — or, as Bishop John Robinson interprets this, 'a righteousness which comes *through* faith in Jesus Christ and *to* all who have such faith'.[8]

This 'righteousness', which was bestowed by God as a free gift — and which thus approximates to 'justification', a word which comes from the same Greek root — was the very core of the gospel. It is not a righteousness which is 'imputed' as a mere legal fiction, nor a righteousness which is instantaneously 'implanted'. It means acquittal, forgiveness and acceptance with God on the basis of the redemption he has himself accomplished — and, of course, the ethical change which this new relationship must of necessity effect.[9] The 'good news' that it conveys did not only, moreover, consist in the liberation it brought to a devout Pharisee like Paul

[3] In *The New Bible Commentary* (ed. J. D. Douglas, Inter-Varsity Press, London, 1962), p. 484.   [4] Galatians 1:11, with 1 Timothy 1:11.
[5] Galatians 1:6-9.   [6] 1 Corinthians 15:3-5.   [7] Romans 1:16 and 17.
[8] Cf. *Wrestling with Romans* (SCM Press, London, 1979), p. 42.
[9] John A. T. Robinson, *op. cit.*, p. 40, partially quoting C. K. Barrett.

himself but in the fact that it was available to literally every type of man. It was not confined to God's covenant people or a matter of Jewish privilege, but was offered just as freely to 'idol worshippers' and those who were 'excluded from citizenship in Israel and foreigners to the covenants of the promise, without hope and without God in the world'[10] – because Christ had 'destroyed the barrier between Jews and everyone else'.[11] It was not limited to the pious, whether by nature or by painstaking perseverance in religious devotions – for he had 'died for the *ungodly*'.[12] Nor was it restricted to those who endeavoured to follow the precepts of morality – for those who were sexually immoral, male prostitutes or homosexual offenders could all share in the justification and 'cleansing' he had died to provide.[13] Nor, again, was this justification conditioned by some change God had already effected in people's lives (such as regeneration, or a new birth; sanctification, or a new moral standard; desire for God, or a new attitude towards him) – for Christ died for us while we were still ungodly, sinners, and even 'enemies' of God, and powerless to do anything about it.[14]

In what, then, does the gospel basically consist? In the good news of a past historical event, in which God in his grace, or wholly unmerited favour, acted on our behalf in Christ when he 'bore our sins in his body on the cross',[15] gave his life 'a ransom for many',[16] and 'was delivered over to death for our sins and was raised to life for our justification'.[17] It is true that this objective act of God in Christ must be appropriated, subjectively, by our reception of it by the empty hand of faith. But the gospel remains the gospel even when men reject it. It is absolutely right and proper – indeed, it is our bounden duty – to plead with men

---

[10] 1 Thessalonians 1:9 and Ephesians 2:12.   [11] Ephesians 2:14.
[12] Romans 5:6;   [13] 1 Corinthians 6:9-11.   [14] Romans 5:6, 8, 10 and
6 again.   [15] 1 Peter 2:24.   [16] Mark 10:45.   [17] Romans 4:25.

and women to receive this good news; but the gospel does not itself consist in people's reception of it, but rather in what they receive. Nor should our reception of this good news by faith be regarded as any sort of contribution which *we* make to our salvation, for Paul states unequivocally that 'it is by grace you have been saved, through faith — and this is not from yourselves, it is the gift of God — not of works, so that no one can boast'.[18] But do the words 'this is the gift of God' refer here to 'faith', to 'saved' or to the whole clause? All these alternatives are possible, but we should probably opt for the last. Hence Barclay translates: 'the whole process comes from nothing we have done or could do', and Skevington Wood comments: 'The element of "giveness" applies to faith as well as grace, for faith is a direct outcome of hearing the saving message'[19] (Romans 10:17).

The relation between the objective proclamation of the gospel and the evangelist's appeal to men to receive it is made clear in Paul's words in 2 Corinthians 5:18-21:

> All this is from God, who reconciled us to himself through Christ and gave us the ministry of reconciliation: that God was reconciling the world to himself in Christ, not counting men's sins against them. And he has committed to us the message of reconciliation. We are therefore Christ's ambassadors, as though God were making his appeal through us — we implore you on Christ's behalf: be reconciled to God. God made him who had no sin to be sin for us, so that in him we might become the righteousness of God.

'Reconciliation' is one of the keywords of the gospel, and

[18] Ephesians 2:8 and 9.   [19] A. Skevington Wood, in his Commentary on Ephesians in *The Expositor's Bible Commentary* (General Editor, Frank E. Gaebelein, Zondervan, Grand Rapids, 1978), Vol. II, p. 36.

Professor James Atkinson's comments on the sense in which it is used could, I think, scarcely be bettered:

> When the sinner's wrong relation to God is thought of in terms of an estrangement or alienation from God, the biblical category is reconciliation — we are reconciled to God (Romans 5:10), and God reconciles us to himself (2 Corinthians 5:18 f.; Ephesians 2:16; Colossians 1:20-22). It is nowhere stated that God is reconciled to us. This has caused many scholars to take the view that reconciliation applies to man's alienation and not God's. This view may represent something less than the whole truth. It is true that man is alienated from God owing to his sin, but it is equally true that this incurs the wrath of God and God's alienation. . . . Reconciliation is more than a mere subjective change in us, and can be explained not in psychological categories but in theological. In other words, the word reconciliation is less about man and more about God.
>
> Two Pauline passages support this emphasis: Romans 5:8-11 and 2 Corinthians 5:18-21. The first passage . . . is about God and the Gospel, not about any change in us: the statement is still true, whatever our reaction. It hinges round God, not man's change of heart. This view is supported by 2 Corinthians 5:19. God was in Christ reconciling the world to himself, not imputing their trespasses unto them. It is clear that both passages are emphasizing the objective activity of God not the subjective activity of the human mind. The thought is pursued to the end of the chapter where the graphic phrase is used that Christ was made sin for us, who knew no sin; that we might be made the righteousness of God in him (2 Corinthians 5:21). Nothing could be more objective than the stark statement that Christ was made sin, though, of course, it is

balanced with the subjective change in us, 'that we
might be made the righteousness of God in him'. It
is equally clear in Romans 5:11 that when Paul speaks
of 'receiving the reconciliation', he is not speaking
about a penitential change of heart in us, but rather
of . . . a gift bestowed and received, a status newly
established. . . .[20]

Here the most appropriate simile seems to be that of an
amnesty decalared by a king in favour of his rebellious subjects. This is the king's objective act, by which he offers
pardon and a new relationship to those who were previously
subject to his condemnation. It signifies, therefore, a *change
of attitude* on his part; and it is now up to his rebellious subjects to accept this amnesty (which would, of course, signify
a *change of heart* on their part). In this simile I have used
the words 'change of attitude' in relation to the king, and
'change of heart' in relation to his subjects, designedly. For
in the reconciliation of sinful men and women to himself no
change of heart is needed on God's part, since the act of
reconciliation, at such infinite cost, is sufficient evidence of
the love which caused him to send his Son 'as an atoning
sacrifice for our sins'; but this reconciliation does involve a
change of attitude – from inevitable alienation to loving
acceptance. On man's part, on the other hand, the need was
for a positive change of heart – from one of rebellion and
enmity to submission and love.

Another key word is 'propitiation', for which 'expiation'
has been substituted in most modern translations. In
classical Greek the relevant root (which occurs in Romans
3:25, 1 John 2:2 and 4:10, Hebrews 2:17 and even Luke
18:13) meant to appease, and this sense of the word has
given rise to the completely false idea of a hostile God being

[20] Article on 'Atonement' (3(d)), in *A Dictionary of Christian Theology*
(ed. Alan Richardson, SCM, London, 1969), p. 21.

appeased by a loving Christ. But the Greek root does not carry this meaning in the Septuagint, which is far more relevant to our purpose. In any case its use in 1 John 4:10 should completely dispel any such idea, for this verse makes it clear that the 'propitiation' was initiated by God himself and is the very measure of his love. But this love does not exclude his 'wrath' against the sin which so mars our lives and his fair creation. As Atkinson points out, love and wrath are not contradictory, whereas love and hatred are. In God's wrath there is nothing petty, personal or vindictive. Provided 'expiation' is understood as including this meaning, and 'propitiation' as not conveying any other meaning, it does not seem to me to matter which word is used. Both words, however, need to be explained.

A still more fundamental concept in regard to the gospel is 'justification'. This is basically a forensic term which means to 'acquit'[21] or to 'declare righteous', and is the opposite of 'condemn' or 'pronounce guilty' – as we find in Romans 8:33: 'It is God who justifies. Who is he that condemns?' Hence the phrase 'justification by faith' really means justification by grace alone, in Christ alone, through faith alone. Thus its *source* is the grace, or undeserved favour, of God; for Romans 3:23 states that 'all have sinned and fall short of the glory of God, and are justified freely by his grace through the redemption that came by Christ Jesus'. This leads us on to Christ and his atoning death as the *instrumental basis*, or objective cause, of our justification, for Galatians 2:17 speaks of us being 'justified in Christ'; 1 Corinthians 6:11 of being 'justified in the name of our Lord Jesus Christ'; and Romans 5:9 of being 'justified by his blood' (that is, by his atoning death). Finally, the *subjective medium*, or apprehending cause, of our justification is faith, for in Romans 3:28 Paul states that

---

[21] Or 'give the verdict in favour of'.

'a man is justified by faith apart from observing the law', while in Galatians 2:16 he says that we 'have put our faith in Christ Jesus that we may be justified by faith in Christ Jesus and not by observing the law, because by observing the law no one will be justified'. On this verse Dr J. M. Boice comments that

> in Christ, God declares all righteous who believe, imputing divine righteousness to them. In this sense, justification does not express an ethical change or influence (though ethical changes follow); rather, it expresses the judicial action of God apart from human merit according to which the guilty are pardoned. . . . This experience does not happen automatically to all men. It is true that God justifies, but he does so only as he unites a man or woman to Christ, a union that takes place only through the channel of human faith. Faith is the means, not the source, of justification. Faith is trust. It begins with knowledge, so it is not blind. It builds on facts, so it is not speculation. It stakes its life on the outcome, so it is not impractical. Faith is trusting Christ. The expression in the middle of v. 16, literally 'we have believed *into* Christ', implies an act of personal commitment, not just assenting to the facts concerning Christ, but actually running to him for refuge and seeking mercy.[22]

In the context the point at issue was, of course, whether a man might be 'justified' simply by throwing himself, in naked faith, on Christ and his atoning death without placing any reliance on his own attempts to observe the Mosaic law — either as a means of salvation or an integral and necessary element in God's covenant of grace with Israel. In wider terms, however, the way of salvation for all

---

[22] J. M. Boice, 'Galatians', in *The Expositor's Bible Commentary*, Vol. 10, pp. 448 f.

men is at stake. Is this to be earned by obedience, or accepted as a gift? And are we to try to do God's will in order to win his acceptance, or as our grateful response to an acceptance already freely bestowed?

What, then, is the true function of 'the law' — and, more fundamentally still, what precisely are we to understand by this term, in a spiritual sense, today? To the Jew, as we have seen, it meant the *Torah*, which represented the whole corpus of teaching and instruction given by God to his covenant people. This was largely centred, as Dr Stuart Blanch has insisted,[23] on the Ten Commandments, and the more detailed precepts, ordinances and exhortations that may be regarded as flowing from them. But I have already suggested that, in the light of the way in which Christ may be said not to have abolished, but rather *fulfilled* the Mosaic Law, it seems to me that the distinction made in the seventh of the Thirty-Nine Articles between those precepts which can be classified as moral, ceremonial and civil, respectively, is of great importance. The Puritans, too, commonly made the same distinction when they divided the Mosaic Law, in a slightly different order, into the moral, the judicial and the ceremonial law — and with precisely the same implications: namely, that the judicial law, as the civil law of Israel, was no longer of direct relevance to Christian life; that the ceremonial law, largely concerned with the Levitical institution of priesthood and sacrifice, had been finally fulfilled by the saving work of Christ; but that the moral law, founded on the character of God himself, had abiding significance — although as a pattern of life, rather than a legal code.[24] But what can we say in this context about men of other religions — and particularly those who totally deny the existence of a personal God?

[25] *The Trumpet in the Morning*, cf. pp. 48 ff. above. [24] Cf. E. F. Kevan, *The Grace of Law* (London, 1964), pp. 43, 63, etc. (with footnote references).

Without going into any further details — which have been discussed, to some degree, in the previous chapters of this book — about the beliefs professed today by men of different schools of thought in some of the great world religions, I have no doubt that the Bible teaches that men of all religions or no religion have *some* knowledge of this basic moral law. The vast majority, for example, would join in an 'affirmation of law as a dimension in the universe and as a dimension of man's spiritual life'[25] (provided the word 'spiritual' is given its widest significance), and they would express the social implications of this law in terms of certain basic human rights. I cannot myself believe that, when St Paul wrote:

> Indeed, when the Gentiles, who do not have the [Mosaic] law, do by nature things required by the law, they are a law for themselves, even though they do not have the law, since they show that the requirements of the law are written on their hearts, their consciences also bearing witness, and their thoughts now accusing, now even defending them[26]

he was thinking of the New Covenant rather than a basic apprehension of the requirements of the moral law implanted in man as man. Here I agree with Anthony Burgess's statement that

> You must not, with Austine, compare this place with that gracious promise in Jeremy, of God writing his law on the hearts of his people. There is therefore a two-fold writing in the hearts of men; the first, of knowledge and judgement, whereby they apprehend what is good and bad: the second is in the will and affections,

---

[25] H. J. Berman, *op. cit.*, p. 101.   [26] Romans 2:14 and 15. It is, however, distinctly possible that the words 'by nature' should be taken with the preceding clause ('have the law') rather than the word 'do'.

by giving a propensity and delight, with some measure
of strength, to do this upon good grounds.[27]
Nor can I agree with Jacques Ellul when he states that the
doctrine of a continuing knowledge of the law of God is
'built upon a single text';[28] for the same basic principle seems
to underlie Romans 1:32 and a number of other passages.[29]

Now it is true, of course, that the Puritans rightly insisted
that man's knowledge of, and ability to keep, this basic
moral law had been vastly affected by the Fall. But they
believed that 'neither of these harmful results was complete
or absolute, and that there was sufficient evidence to show
that man still had some knowledge of the Law and that he
still possessed a measure of ability'.[30] Other Protestant
theologians have explained this knowledge and ability in
terms of the doctrine of 'Common Grace'. P. S. Watson,
moreover, states that, in his view, what is commonly called
'Natural Law' means

> that God's law is written in life before it is ever written
> anywhere else, and particular formulations of it (such
> as the Decalogue or the Golden Rule) arise out of the
> realities of human existence. For God and our God-
> given neighbours are still there, making ceaseless
> demands on us by just being there, so we cannot escape
> them even if in our sinfulness we are blind to their true
> meaning.[31]

Precisely the same is true, Paul teaches, in regard to men's
knowledge of the very existence of God himself. For he states
unequivocally in Romans 1:19-23 that

> what may be known about God is plain to them,

---

[27] Kevan, *op. cit.*, p. 59 – quoting from *Vindicae Legis*, p. 60.   [28] *The
Theological Foundations of Law* (English Translation, London, 1961),
p. 45.   [29] Cf. C. H. Dodd, *Natural Law in the Bible* (London, 1946),
and passages such as Matthew 7:11; Romans 12:17; 1 Peter 2:12 and 3:16.
[30] Kevan, *op. cit.*, p. 69.   [31] Article on 'Law' in *A Dictionary of Christian Theology*, p. 190.

because God has made it plain to them. For since the creation of the world God's invisible qualities – his eternal power and divine nature – have been clearly seen, being understood from what has been made, so that men are without excuse. For although they knew God, they neither glorified him as God nor gave thanks to him, but their thinking became futile and their foolish hearts were darkened. Although they claimed to be wise, they became fools and exchanged the glory of the immortal God for images made to look like mortal man and birds and animals and reptiles.

This is an exposition of what is commonly termed 'general revelation'. It constitutes, of course, an essentially limited testimony when compared with God's 'special revelation' in the Bible (and, supremely, in Christ), for it 'reflects God in certain aspects only – namely, "his eternal power and divine nature".'[32] Even so, millions of men have, down the ages, 'suppressed' this truth in favour either of their own philosophy or some idolatrous form of religious thought and practice.

This is a very sombre picture. But it does, at least, provide some real encouragement to us to proclaim both the law and the love of God even to those who deny his existence and ignore what he has revealed of his nature and will. For it means that, underneath their repudiation of this revelation, there is something to which the message of his law and love can appeal. This may be so overlaid by centuries of traditional thought and practice as to be almost dead; but the Holy Spirit can still quicken it. It is this, I think, that the apostle Paul had in mind when he wrote:

> The weapons we fight with are not the weapons of the world. On the contrary, they have divine power to

[32] Everett F. Harrison, in his Commentary on Romans, *The Expositor's Bible Commentary*, Vol. 10, p. 23.

demolish strongholds. We demolish arguments and
every pretension that sets itself up against the
knowledge of God . . .[33]

And precisely the same applies also to all those who, without
actually denying the existence of a personal God or the
mission of Christ, in practice ignore both.

So much for what is meant in this context by 'law',
whether used with or without the definite article. In all the
passages that have been quoted the meaning is either the
basic moral law of God or the Mosaic legislation as such. But
what, precisely, are the *functions* of the law? It was certainly
never intended to be a way of salvation, as is evident from
Paul's categorical statement in Romans 3:20 that 'no one
will be declared righteous in [God's] sight by observing the
law'. But Dr E. F. Kevan states that it

> has been traditional in post-Reformation theology to
> speak of the three uses of the Law – *usus politicus*, to
> restrain sin; *usus pedagogus*, to lead to Christ; and
> *usus normativus*, to determine the believer's conduct.
> Lutherans and Calvinists concur in these three, but
> differ slightly in the stress they lay on the *usus
> normativus*.[34]

In this context we can, I think, ignore the *usus politicus*,
except to refer again[35] to 1 Timothy 1:9 and 10, to such
books as A. R. Vidler's *Christ's Strange Work*[36] and to the
exhortation in Romans 11:22 to consider both 'the kindness
and sternness of God'. But the *usus pedagogus* is implicit in
the second part of Romans 3:20, which reads: 'rather,
through the law we become conscious of sin'; and Paul
elsewhere testifies from his own experience that

> I would not have known what it was to covet if the law
> had not said 'Do not covet'. But sin, seizing the

---

[33] 2 Corinthians 10:4 f.   [34] *Op. cit.*, p. 38.   [35] Cf. p. 133 above.
[36] SCM Press, London, Revised ed., 1963.

opportunity afforded by the commandment, produced in me every kind of covetous desire . . . Did that which is good, then, become death to me? By no means! But in order that sin might be recognized as sin, it produced death in me through what was good, so that through the commandment sin might become utterly sinful.[37]

That the law – and its proclamation – should in fact exercise this function seems to me essential; for the offer of a full and free forgiveness from the guilt of sin, and of deliverance from God's 'wrath', is almost meaningless to those who have no sense of the one and no fear of the other. Otherwise there would be a grave danger that the proclamation of 'free grace' would degenerate into what has justly been termed 'cheap grace'. This purpose behind the moral law is, moreover, clearly stated in one of the two possible translations of Galatians 3:24: namely, 'so the law was put in charge [or was our "child-custodian"] to lead us to Christ that we might be justified by faith' – for the man who is truly convicted of sin knows well that there is no other way of salvation or assurance of divine forgiveness. In this context it becomes clear that the Sermon on the Mount, far from constituting the heart of the Gospel (as some people fondly imagine), should be regarded as the apex of the Law. It is true that the ethical teaching of Jesus does not represent a set of rules so much as a 'number of illustrations of the way in which a transformed character will express itself in conduct';[38] but it throws into bold relief both the standard of life the 'law of God' really requires and the utter impossibility that anyone could ever measure up to it.

I have, however, already quoted Dr Kevan's statement that the Reformers differed somewhat in their view of the third use of the moral law – namely, as a pattern of conduct

---

[37] Romans 7:7, 8 and 13.   [38] T. W. Manson, *The Teaching of Jesus* (Cambridge University Press, 1951), p. 301.

(as distinct from a way of salvation) by which a Christian can — and should — be guided and which he can use as a test of his spiritual progress. Calvin put a major emphasis on this, and

> made it the foundation of his doctrine of sanctification. He held that it was the office of the Law to remind believers of their duty, and thereby to excite them to the pursuit of holiness and integrity. He considered that the principal use of the Law was to instruct believers in the way of spiritual life. . . .[39]

There is considerable doubt, however, whether Luther accepted this use of the law at all, although Dr Kevan quotes H. H. Kramm as stating

> I think it is clearly implied in his writings and teaching that the Law still has some value for the believer. . . . I would say: it is like a compass, indicating the general direction of a journey, not like a detailed map prescribing certain roads.[40]

It is in this context, moreover, that Kevan quotes J. S. Whale's conclusion that 'Whereas Luther distinguishes Law and Gospel and ever gives the pre-eminence to the latter, Calvin unites them; sometimes he comes near to transforming the Gospel into a new Law'.[41]

It is the proper distinction between law and gospel which enables the Christian to steer a middle course between the Scilla of legalism and the Charybdis of antinomianism. This is why Luther affirmed that this 'distinction between Law and Gospel is the highest art in Christendom which should be grasped and understood by all who call themselves

---

[39] Kevan, *op. cit.*, p. 39.   [40] *Ibid.*, p. 38 f., quoting from *Theology of Martin Luther* (London, 1947), p. 61.   [41] *Ibid.*, quoting from *Protestant Tradition* (Cambridge, 1955), p. 164.

Christians. . . . So much depends on this distinction'.[42] As Dr
Alec Vidler has emphasized, there is a close correspondence
   between the redemption of the old Israel from bondage
   in Egypt and the redemption of the new Israel from
   bondage to the Law, a correspondence which is reproduced in the continuing Acts of the Messiah in the
   Apostolic Church unto this day. In the first case, we
   have (1) the bondage in Egypt, (2) the sacrifice of the
   Passover, (3) the miracle of the exodus, followed by (4)
   the giving of the Old Law at Sinai. In the second case
   we have (1) the Messiah's voluntary submission to, and
   fulfilment of, the Old Law which is our bondage, (2)
   the sacrifice of the Cross at the Feast of the Passover,
   (3) the miracle of the Resurrection, followed by (4) the
   giving of the New Law, the grace of the Holy Ghost, at
   Pentecost.[43]

That is why, to the Christian, the law of God is no longer an
external set of commandments which challenge an unwilling, and even impossible, obedience, but the gracious will of
his Saviour God which is now inscribed, internally, on his
heart and mind. As for the gospel, this assures us that

   He who did not spare his own Son, but gave him up for
   us all — how will he not also, along with him, graciously
   give us all things?. . . . Who shall separate us from the
   love of Christ? Shall trouble or hardship or persecution
   or famine or nakedness or danger or sword?. . . . No, in
   all these things we are more than conquerors through
   him who loved us. For I am convinced that neither
   death nor life, neither angels nor demons, neither the
   present nor the future, nor any powers, neither height
   nor depth, nor anything else in all creation, will be

[42] Cf. R. D. Preus, article on 'Law and Gospel', in *Baker's Dictionary of
Christian Ethics* (ed. Carl F. H. Henry, Baker Book House, Michigan,
1973), pp. 379 ff.; M. J. Heineken, in *A Dictionary of Christian Ethics*,
p. 193.   [43] *Op. cit.*, p. 59.

able to separate us from the love of God that is in
Christ Jesus our Lord.[44]
It is the Incarnation – which includes, of course, the Atonement and Resurrection – which has changed everything, for
Christ not only fulfilled God's law but died to liberate us
from the 'curse' it pronounces, on all those who have not
kept it fully, by 'becoming a curse for us'.[45] So it is he who
assures us, in a wholly unique way, of God's love.

It seems to me, then, that the major points which, when
taken together, distinguish the Christian faith from all other
faiths are, first, that Christian worship sees God as not only
personal but essentially as 'Love'. Secondly, that he is also
'Light' – or shining, unclouded holiness – which means that
his love is never mawkish or sentimental, but 'a consuming
fire'. Thirdly, that his love and his holiness meet, and find
their supreme manifestation, at the Cross (which, far from
'assuaging an irate deity', represents the essential moral
basis on which God can, and does, do away with that alienation 'which sin brings and which compels men to know his
love as wrath').[46] Only so could he 'demonstrate his justice'
in acquitting and accepting all who turn to him in repentance and faith.[47] Fourthly, that this redemption was infi-
nitely costly, for it was not only the incarnate Son who
suffered but also the Father who sent him. Fifthly, that
Christ's resurrection and exaltation mean that we do not
follow a dead prophet but worship, and seek to obey, a
living Saviour who is eternally one with the Father and the
Holy Spirit in the unity of the triune Godhead (for only one
who was truly divine could redeem us from sin), but is also
still man. So he is able both to understand us and to meet
our every need.

Finally, I will let a very learned Muslim, Dr Daud
Rahbar, speak for himself in a few extracts from a circular

[44] Romans 8:32, 35 and 37 ff.   [45] Galatians 3:10 and 13.   [46] John
Robinson, *op. cit.*, p 45.   [47] Romans 3:26.

letter he sent to his Muslim friends in 1960 to explain why he
had 'become a Christian'. He wrote:

> Allow me to ask you: What is the disposition of God
> towards his human creatures according to Islam? Is He
> a merciful God? Is He only an angry God? Or is He
> both? If He is both, is He so in a capricious way or a
> judicious way? Is He a Sovereign of strict justice? Or do
> you wish to dismiss the whole subject of divine disposi-
> tion by declaring the *bi lā kayf* formula,[48] meaning,
> 'We do not know *how*. God is the transcendent and the
> incomprehensible. His ways we know not'.
>
> If you choose this last answer (which is implicit in much
> of Muslim theology), are you not explaining away a
> whole mass of Qur'anic verses which speak of God's
> mercy, love, retribution and avenging in various ways?
> Almost every third verse in the Qur'ān speaks of God as
> the Lord of Justice who will reward and punish on the
> Judgement Day. . . .
>
> To say, 'We do not know if and how God punishes and
> rewards and avenges and shows mercy and loves, for
> His ways transcend our understanding', is to dismiss
> the entire subject of a divine character. Moreover such
> a dismissal is only nominal, for in thinking of God as
> transcendent in the sense of incomprehensible, one
> evades specifying divine morality and ends up by
> believing in His inscrutable and unpredictable will. . . .
>
> Let us think without any bias: To sane human intellect
> anywhere in the world certainly justice is a necessary
> attribute of the Sovereign Creator. But what should
> truly divine justice mean?
>
> Think of the Creator-God in two ways:
> (1) The Creator says to Himself: 'I am going to create
> mankind. On earth they will have sickness, anxiety,

[48] Cf. pp. 101 f. above.

fear, social wrongs, infidelities of fortune and fellow-beings, deaths of loved ones, disappointments, toils, and then when they die I shall reward and punish them strictly. This is my justice.'

(2) Think of the Creator-God then in another way: He says to Himself, 'I am going to create the world that I may have fellowship with man. . . . I shall myself go and live a span of earthly human life and disclose directly to men that I am with them in their suffering. In that earthly life I shall suffer literally the *worst* of suffering by dying the worst death of human violence.'

Which of the above justices is superior? That wherein the Creator Himself sits eternally on the Heavenly Throne, from eternity waiting for the Judgement Day when He will sit in judgement on his creatures and reward and punish with stringent equity? Or that justice wherein the Creator Himself is no less a recipient of what He gives to His creatures?

This transcendent justice of God is only another name for His love for men. Only in love does justice transcend itself and become loving sacrifice: *giving what is due and then giving more.* . . .

Mankind has existed for countless generations. In our search for the truly worshipable, we must therefore look in human history for a man who loved, who lived humbly like the poorest, who was perfectly innocent and sinless, who was tortured and humiliated in *literally the worst* manner, and who declared his continued transparent love for those who had inflicted the worst of injuries on him. If we do find such a man, He must be the Creator-God Himself. For if the Creator-God Himself is not that Supremely Suffering and Loving Man, then the Creator-God is provenly inferior to that Man. And this cannot be. . . .

Such a man did live on earth nearly two thousand years ago. His name was Jesus. . . . When I read the New Testament and discovered how Jesus loved and forgave His killers from the Cross, I could not fail to recognize that the love He had for men is the only kind of love worthy of the Eternal God.

Once more I say: If the innocent Jesus, who forgave and loved His crucifiers from the Cross, was not the Creator-God Himself, then the Creator-God is proven to be inferior to Jesus. And this cannot be.

The Creator-God and Jesus are one and the same Being. May all men know that truly divine love.

This is not, of course, the full doctrine of the Atonement, but it sums up, very clearly, some of the essential — and unique — features of the gospel.

Index of Authors

(whose works are quoted or cited in this book)

N.B. Details about the books concerned can be found in the footnotes on the relevant pages.

Index of Names
(Persons, Places, Sects, Schools of Thought
Doctrines, Encyclopedias, etc.)

Index of Technical Terms

198